SOFTWARE AS A SCIENCE

SAAS ACADEMY
Press

SOFTWARE
AS A
SCIENCE

Unlock Limitless Recurring Revenue
Without Losing Control

DAN
MARTELL

MATT
VERLAQUE

JOHNNY
PAGE

MARCEL
PETITPAS

Foreword by Patrick Campbell, Founder of ProfitWell

SAAS ACADEMY
Press

A SaaS Academy Press Book
www.SaaSAcademy.com
Software As A Science © Copyright 2024 SaaS Growth Coach Inc
By Dan Martell, Matt Verlaque, Johnny Page, Marcel Petitpas
First Edition

Published in the United States by SaaS Academy Press
in collaboration with Stone Crest Books
Stone Crest | www.StoneCrestBooks.com

For more information, visit www.saasacademy.com

ISBN Identifiers:
978-1-961462-30-4   (Hardcover)
978-1-961462-29-8   (Paperback)
978-1-961462-31-1   (eBook)
978-1-961462-32-8   (Audiobook)

To all the visionary SaaS founders who came before, thank you for blazing the trail. We're all standing on the shoulders of giants.

To all the mentors who taught us, coached us, challenged us, and molded us: thank you for being so generous with your time and experience. We wouldn't be here without you.

To our families: thank you for supporting all of our crazy dreams and inspiring us to think bigger than we ever thought possible.

To the team at SaaS Academy, past and present: thank you for working tirelessly to build the best coaching program in the world and to support our clients in every way possible.

To the small group of advance readers who gave us early feedback: thank you for being so generous with your time and opinions. It's easy to say "great job" and move on, but instead, you truly helped make this book better.

But most importantly...

To the founders who have come through our doors over the years—this book was built by you just as much as it was by us. Without you—tirelessly building, testing, challenging yourselves, and growing incredible businesses—it would be a volume of empty pages.

We're incredibly grateful for the opportunity to serve such a brilliant and hardworking group of clients. It's a privilege that most people could only dream of.

Above all else...this book is for you.

— Dan, Matt, Johnny, and Marcel

Contents

Foreword

FOUNDING AND RUNNING A successful SaaS company is hard. Really hard. There are cash flow hurdles, marketing hurdles, and (my favorite topic) pricing hurdles. *Opinions* on how to solve these hurdles are pretty easy to find (just Google them). But *proven* answers you can trust are a lot harder to come by. Welcome to a book that cuts through the noise with data, stories, and proven answers you can trust.

For most of my professional life, I've been on a mission to help software founders unlock the strategies that *work*. That work led me to founding ProfitWell, before it was acquired by Paddle, where I served as the CSO.

Software as a Science delivers on a number of the most difficult problems facing our industry: sales, marketing, retention, and pricing. Dan, Matt, Johnny, and Marcel don't just write down the answers; they *show* you how to apply them to your own software company.

Here's what you need to know about this book:

1: *Every* SaaS Founder Can Use These Strategies

We can debate all day long about the best strategies for growing a SaaS company. But facts are hard to argue. Right from chapter one, you'll find convincing evidence from tons of analyses on how certain elements underpin *every SaaS company on Earth* — acquisition, retention, and expansion. Increase one, increase your chances of success. Fail at one, and your company will likely fail with it.

2: The Authors *Prove* Their Frameworks

I've sat in the room with all of these guys. I've spoken on their stages at SaaS Academy events with hundreds of SaaS founders from across the globe. We've discussed how to handle product-market fit, uncovered marketing tactics, and digested complex problems to find the simple answers. In this book, the authors draw on these experiences and provide examples from real SaaS companies just like yours that have used tactics such as their Ultimate Price-Increase Method, the Rocket Demo Builder, and other frameworks. Not opinions, just results. And the stories to prove it.

3: They Deliver Detailed Frameworks with Simple Next Steps

At the end of the day, without some straightforward takeaways, elegant solutions are nothing more than pipe dreams. I love how Dan, Matt, Johnny, and Marcel put this book together — they offer detailed analyses of their frameworks, and then, at the end of every chapter, they offer you *the next steps you can take immediately.*

Let's take one of my favorite sections, chapter 6. In this part of the book, they address the churn problem that happens if you don't have a strong activation process. First, the chapter unpacks a specific, detailed plan that they've used with *hundreds* of other companies to cut churn in half. Then, at the end of the chapter, they give you the three simple next steps you can do (literally *in the book, as you're reading)* to get a jumpstart on fixing your product activation *now.*

Here's what you need to understand: this book has the stories to pull you in, the data to convince you, and the results to prove that the models work. If you're in SaaS or, honestly, *any* recurring revenue business, this is a must-have resource. Get it. Read it. Pass it on to your team.

—Patrick Campbell, founder of ProfitWell

Introduction

"HOP IN."

Dan called Marcel on the phone, asking if he wanted to go for a run. About thirty seconds after Marcel said "sure," he heard the rumbling engine of Dan's supercar. In typical Dan Martell style, he was already waiting outside Marcel's house. *Hop in.*

They drove to the trailhead, parked the car, and jogged. Just as Marcel was getting out of breath, Dan shared why he was *really* so eager to go on this run. He wanted Marcel to be the first-ever expert coach at SaaS Academy. SaaS Academy was growing quickly under Dan's leadership, and there were more and more founders showing up in the community ready to scale their companies—which meant there were more people to help than Dan could handle by himself. And Marcel kept following Dan's lead.

It was 2016, and at the time, the software world was falling over itself looking for venture capital funds. You were more likely to hear people bragging about *raising* money than you were to hear people talking about *making* money. Investors had deep pockets, and they were all looking for the next unicorn. Software founders, intoxicated by the thought of huge investment rounds, gravitated toward raising cash as the default model for company building. It was almost like the investors became their customers, and their funding requests became their sales pitches. The game was no longer about creating the best product for the right customers and then iterating toward perfection—it was about "growth at all costs" and making sure that you could raise your next round at a higher valuation than the last one.

We're not bashing venture capital funding—it has its place. Dan raised venture capital for his last two companies before SaaS Academy. And he, in turn, has invested in dozens of other businesses as an angel investor. Raising venture capital is a great tool for the right type of business. In fact, for those businesses, it's likely the only tool that'll work. But in our opinion, it's a tool that gets misapplied to lots of companies that don't really need it.

When Dan said, "Hop in," he wasn't just inviting Marcel into a car. He was inviting Marcel to join what would become the most successful coaching program in the world for B2B SaaS founders, and to work with some of the most incredible software CEOs of the last two decades. And those two little words embodied the same type of invitation that Dan used to hook Johnny and Matt—the other two authors of this book—to join the company a few years later. So, we find it only fitting that we offer the same invitation to you:

Hop in.

The Back Story

SaaS Academy was created with the goal of helping SaaS founders who had reached their first $10,000 in monthly recurring revenue (MRR) learn how to scale their company, deliver results for their customers, and build a business that they wouldn't grow to hate.

But that vision—with its tight target market and highly specific mission—didn't arise out of nowhere. That vision was born the way most entrepreneurs birth a new company: first by seeing a problem without a solution, and then by building the solution.

Software had been second nature to Dan for years before he founded SaaS Academy. After a troubled childhood and a number of run-ins with the law, he found himself in a rehab facility staring at an old computer and a dusty yellow book about Java programming. He cracked the book, fired up the machine, punched a few keys, and as soon as he saw "Hello World!" appear on the screen...he was *hooked*. After a couple of early failures, he found success with his company Spheric Technologies, which went on to sell for millions. A few years later, he started Flowtown, which was acquired by Demandforce in 2011. The term "serial entrepreneur" was starting to fit.

In 2012, Dan started Clarity.fm—a software platform that helped entrepreneurs get advice over the phone from *people who had the answers*. This was a platform for any entrepreneur in any business anywhere in the world. Not sure how to fix your empty sales funnel? Clarity has someone who's done it. No idea which side of your marketplace to solve for first? There's an expert on Clarity. Don't know how to set up your pitch deck to go raise that money you need? You get the idea.

The network of experts that jumped on to serve others with their expertise was incredible—from serial entrepreneurs, to nine-figure-CEOs, to some of the most talented sales and marketing voices in the world...most of them were on Clarity.fm sharing their genius with the people who needed it most. And Dan had a front-row seat, which helped his mission become clearer: he was here on Earth to connect entrepreneurs with the knowledge they need. Although Clarity was a great start, it still felt like he was hitting just outside the bullseye. After Clarity was acquired in 2015, Dan's mission became even more focused:

It was time to build a community that has all the answers...<u>only for B2B SaaS founders.</u>

Dan knew that most of the communities and accelerators for SaaS founders were born out of the echo chamber of raising venture capital in order to grow—and that many of these communities weren't as interested in helping founders build durable revenue as they were interested in helping them raise capital. Where was the authoritative resource for those who wanted to start their own business, and run it themselves? Where was the group that showed bootstrappers that they can create a big company—or even become a unicorn—*without* relying on venture capitalist dollars?

That group didn't exist. So, Dan did what any self-respecting serial entrepreneur would do—he built the solution: a program just for B2B SaaS founders, where coaching, content, and community could all come together to help as many founders as humanly possible.

And just like that, it was off to the races. Built on Dan's incredible network of the smartest minds in SaaS, the business took off. Anyone who wanted to learn how to increase their revenue, reduce their churn, or fix their product positioning was joining. And that growth was what led up to Dan and Marcel going for that run—and to Marcel joining SaaS Academy.

Dan was an early investor in Marcel's company Parakeeto, which helps digital agencies run more profitably. Marcel wouldn't tell you this himself, so the rest of us will let you know: Parakeeto is a world-class example of how a tech-enabled services business should work—it's thriving under Marcel's leadership. So, it makes sense why Dan brought Marcel into SaaS Academy: His ability to quickly understand complex problems, ask challenging questions, and reframe the solution in its simplest form...it's uncanny to the rest of us. By now, he's done thousands of coaching calls with B2B SaaS founders, helping them market their companies, understand their numbers, and serve their customers at a world-class level.

In fact, that was the exact type of coaching that attracted Matt and Johnny to join as clients. Sitting at a SaaS Academy event in 2018—in the front row taking lots of notes—is where they met for the first time.

They didn't know each other—Johnny was from the west coast, Matt from the east, running two different companies. But they had many of the same problems. They were both SaaS CEOs, trying to figure out how to scale, and weren't always sure what to do next.

For his part, Johnny had taken over his company from within—he first joined Silvertrac Software as a commission-only sales rep in 2013. By 2015, Silvertrac had increased their revenue to almost $100,000 per month, primarily from the sales that Johnny and his team were bringing in. He then stepped into a leadership role as the head of Customer Success, where he was instrumental in nearly tripling their MRR again. The next stop was the CEO role, when he joined SaaS Academy as a client and guided Silvertrac through its successful acquisition (at an 8x revenue multiple) in November of 2019.

Matt left a successful career as a firefighter to create his company, UpLaunch, in 2017, and joined SaaS Academy as a client the following year. He found himself firmly plateaued—something we know that almost every SaaS founder faces—at $18,000 in MRR, and he wasn't sure how to get past it—but he was incredibly committed to figuring it out.

The biggest advantage Matt had was that he is a ruthless implementor—he and his team installed playbook after playbook from SaaS Academy (one per week for the first twelve weeks), fought hard for their customers, and ended up rebuilding most of the business. After those first twelve weeks, UpLaunch enjoyed double digit growth every single month until he and his co-founders sold the company for over a 10x revenue multiple in January of 2020.

You might have noticed that Johnny and Matt exited their companies at almost the same time...which meant that those two CEOs who were once sitting in the front row taking notes would soon be looking for their next adventure. And that adventure would be with Dan and Marcel at SaaS Academy.

By then, the word was out—just like at Clarity, experts from around the world were joining as speakers at our in-person events and coaching founders in our weekly sessions. These experts—people like Patrick Campbell (founder of ProfitWell) and Simon Bowen (creator of The Models Method)—combined with Dan and the SaaS Academy coaching team, had built an incredible library of cutting-edge growth playbooks, and an incredible community to help with implementation. And people kept asking the question:

"When are you guys finally going to write a book??"

Here's the thing: we weren't really writers. Sure, most of us had a blog, and SaaS Academy had thousands and thousands of hours of content (enough to write an actual encyclopedia). But no one had ever accused us of being authors. We were founders, coaches, creators, and mentors...but none of us had the first clue how to write a book.

And besides—there was a lot to do. Johnny and Matt both held C-level positions in SaaS Academy and were laser-focused on delivering results for our clients. Marcel was still coaching, while also scaling his company Parakeeto (not to mention running his podcast and speaking at events as well).

But everything changed when Dan released his own book, *Buy Back Your Time*, in 2022. It became a *Wall Street Journal* bestseller, old-school style: organically. While that book was for *all* entrepreneurs—showing them how they can get their time back—it sparked the same community to ask us again, "Where's the SaaS book?"

> **Create world-class training and share it with the world.**

That's one of our mantras at SaaS Academy. And although we've done that to a certain extent with our marketing and YouTube content. . . we finally agreed that after seven years of running SaaS Academy and helping thousands of founders, it was time to write the book.

Most people don't realize the depth of what actually goes on inside of SaaS Academy. There's a full-time team of Executive Coaches that can use a mathematical formula to predict exactly when your company will stop growing. We've refined our content library into about 300 best-in-class playbooks to help founders cure whatever is holding them back. And our sales demo process has been used by our clients to sell over *one billion dollars in software* since we first started teaching it (more on that in chapter 5).

Inside this book, you'll find everything you need to know to run one of the worlds' greatest SaaS companies. While anyone could find this book useful—as many of the tactics are time-tested and based on sound business principles—we wrote this book specifically for the founders who already have a SaaS company, who are wanting to know how to scale it, the right way, with *less* frustration and *more* financial reward. If you've got a B2B SaaS company—whether you're at $1 million MRR, or you haven't even launched yet—this book is for you. It's the last book you'll ever need to read when it comes to understanding how your business works, breaking through your revenue plateaus, and making the right moves *at the right time* in order to unlock growth.

It's all about what's true, not what's new.

The foundational playbooks of the SaaS Academy curriculum don't talk about shiny objects and cutting-edge technology. We don't care if what we say is sexy or not. We're too pragmatic for that. In fact, most of these playbooks are timeless, built around the patterns of business that never change: creating a point of view in the market, generating sales conversations and converting them into customers, onboarding and retaining those customers, creating raving fans, and nailing your pricing and packaging.

The strategies in each chapter of this book have helped to create hundreds of success stories, dozens of incredible exits, and a tribe of founders who have finally realized that they don't need to choose between scaling their company and living the lifestyle they've always dreamed of.

Most of these strategies have been kept private for our clients...until now. But all four of us agree—it's finally time to give our best playbooks to the world.

Why? Because the software landscape has drastically changed.

The capital investment required to start a SaaS company is a fraction of what it once was. More people are starting software companies every single day. The competition for venture capital is tougher than ever—the days of raising a seed round from a slide deck at a $5 million valuation are long gone. The result? More and more founders are building companies without having to clear the hurdle of raising capital in order to get started.

The easier it is to start a company...the harder it's going to be to grow it. The internet is getting more crowded, and marketing channels are noisier than they were even two years ago. Today's reality is clear:

> **Your competitive advantage isn't how you write your code. It's how you serve your customers.**

***

Many things have changed since the early days of SaaS Academy. Johnny has taken the reigns as the CEO, and Dan has moved into a chairman role, overseeing his portfolio of businesses. Matt is now COO, supporting Johnny, and Marcel is still at the helm of Parakeeto, growing it to new heights. But the one thing that will never change is our passion and dedication for helping SaaS founders.

This book is a true labor of love. We wrote it four different times (yes, really). We've re-organized it, tweaked it, edited it, changed it, and edited it again. We sketched every model, framework, and graphic on an iPad. We fought over every comma.

The 4 of us spent a full year revisiting all of our best playbooks, strategies, and stories from SaaS Academy and distilled them down into eleven incredible chapters.

And now, you're holding our life's work in your hands.

We only ask one thing in return: If you're a software founder, don't simply read this book and set it down. This is not a "shelf help" book. Every chapter has specific implementation steps at the end—so if you're reading something that solves a problem that you have, take action. Install the playbooks in your business, measure the results, and build the company that you know you deserve.

You can do this. We've done it. We've helped thousands of others do it too.

So, like Dan said to Marcel all those years ago. . . "Hop in."

We're rooting for you.

—Dan, Matt, Johnny, and Marcel

CHAPTER 1

Your SaaS Company Tastes Like Chicken. . . and It's Supposed To

"You may think your business is unique...but trust me. It's not."[i]
NOAH KAGAN, founder and CEO of AppSumo and author of
New York Times bestseller *Million Dollar Weekend*

EIGHTEEN MONTHS OF DEDICATION. A year and a half of late nights, working hard, and working *harder*. And still...no growth.

Maybe I should go back to firefighting.

A few miles away, Matt's former firefighting crew was either saving lives fighting a blaze, or in the downtime they had, kicking back at the firehouse he used to call home. There, at Station 4—a busy firehouse in Arlington, Virginia—Matt had worked, trained, and been promoted to Lieutenant a year earlier. Now, he wasn't saving anyone's life. He wasn't searching for people trapped in a house fire or dangling from a rope. He wasn't cooking big firehouse dinners or working out in between calls. He'd walked away from all of it to start this company. Instead of living the firehouse life he'd spent a decade in, now he was fighting a new kind of fire—one that had been blazing for eighteen months—and none of it was extinguished.

Matt and Jake—a Marine-turned-firefighter whom Matt met while working together at Station 4—had started a business (almost) accidentally. Besides working as a firefighter, Jake also owned his own gym. Matt was a bit of a "secret nerd"—and he helped Jake with his gym's website and marketing strategy as he was getting going. Then, in 2015, they'd taken that same marketing playbook that had worked for Jake's gym and offered it to others. The playbook caught the eye of Chris Cooper, founder of Two-Brain Business (one of the premier mentorship programs in the world for gym owners). So, Chris brought Jake on his podcast so he could give away that same gym marketing playbook for free, along with a done-for-you version for $99. *Sure would be cool if a dozen gyms actually paid us for this*, Matt and Jake thought.

Three days later, a hundred gyms had signed up.

Matt and Jake used that initial traction to pre-sell gym owners on their upcoming software platform, UpLaunch, which would deliver professional marketing strategies to bring in new leads and retain existing members. Within six months of going live, UpLaunch had over fifty customers on board, and in another six months, they arrived at $18,000 in ongoing, monthly revenue from those customers, or what we call *MRR* in the SaaS world. Sounds good, right? $18,000 in ongoing, monthly revenue within twelve months?

The problem was. . . they were at exactly the same place *another* year and a half later. It took twelve months to build what seemed like a rocket ship of a business, and just one more month to completely flatline it. Sure, new customers were still coming on board, but just as many were leaving. Customer in, customer out. Instead of a rocket ship, they'd just built the world's most frustrating hamster wheel.

At the time, Matt didn't have a name for what UpLaunch was experiencing (at least not one our editor would let us repeat in the book), but little did he know that their company's problems were so predictable, there's actually an official name for it—a Growth Ceiling.

> **When your company is adding and losing the same number of customers, you've hit your Growth Ceiling. And it sucks.**

Ever hit a similar point in your business? When it feels as if no matter how hard you fight, the revenue won't seem to tick upward? It's frustrating as hell—especially for founders who've built, brick by painful brick (or line of code by painstaking line of code) a true business that has a real product for real customers. Regardless of whether you're just starting, or you've got a fifty-person team, your next Growth Ceiling is looming. And when you hit it, it's a crushing feeling—because you can't just outwork it. Instead of your effort creating more growth, it just feels like you're treading water. You're expending even more emotional energy for the same thing you had yesterday, and it feels like you can barely keep your head above the waves—but you certainly aren't surfing them.

Matt and Jake—maybe like you—had already turned their backs on their successful careers, left their retirement funds on the table, and sacrificed a major part of their identities as firefighters when they dove headfirst into entrepreneurship. Neither of them had taken a salary. Both had contributed tens of thousands of dollars into the business. And all that helped accelerate their company's growth. . . until it got to $18,000 MRR.

These guys weren't dummies. They noticed the growth stall—and to fix it, they tried new and exciting marketing tactics. They took on new channel partners. They tinkered with their product. Still, nothing was working, and it was getting scary, and, by the middle of 2018, UpLaunch was only a few months from having to close up shop.

This was one blaze these two firefighting pros couldn't seem to put out.

Your Company Is a Math Problem

After coaching thousands of founders from around the world in SaaS Academy—some who are building their first-ever business and others who have multiple exits under their belts—we can tell you with confidence that the flatline Matt was experiencing happens all the time. The first plateau (for most SaaS companies) usually pops up somewhere between $10,000 and $30,000 in MRR. And the only way through it is to stop brute-forcing growth and start taking a systematic approach to solving the math problem that is your SaaS company.

We'll say it again:

> **Your company is a math problem. And math problems have solutions.**

You might think your business is unique. You might believe that your problems are one-off issues that require creative solutions. You might *feel* like no one on Earth could understand your customers, your product, or your business model.

In reality, your SaaS company—regardless of who you serve, what you deliver, or which tech stack you use—is almost exactly like everyone else's. In fact, it's so similar, we can boil it down to math.

When we say this to founders, they usually get offended. "That's probably true for other companies, but not ours—our company is different, and you just don't understand our market, or our product." Most founders feel like their company is like a little snowflake—every single one is unique. . . right?

Kind of.

Here's the thing about snowflakes—they all look unique, but they're based on a few simple elements. Think back to high school science class for a minute—you were probably taught that no two snowflakes are exactly alike. In fact—and if you're a numbers nerd, you'll love this—scientists estimate that there are 10^{70} *more snowflake possibilities than there are atoms in the entire universe.* Written out, that number looks like this:

10,000,000,000,000,000,000,000,000,000,000,000,000,000,000,000,000,0 00,000,000,000,000,000,000

But even with that astronomical number of unique possibilities, a snowflake is still only composed of three elements. Every single snowflake is an ice crystal, coming from frozen water—two parts hydrogen, one part oxygen. But with those simple elements...you can create incredible variation.

So, in a way, you're right: your business is a snowflake—unique in some ways, but made up of a simple, standardized set of ingredients. And when the ingredients are standardized...it means there's a process that needs to be followed in order to grow.

Dan says it best: "Most companies die from indigestion, not starvation."

In other words, the most common way that founders sabotage their own growth is by jumping from idea to idea—without a scientific approach. You can do the right thing in the wrong order and still fail. You can do a really great job solving a problem that's not actually a problem. You can even "fix" the wrong thing and end up with a worse result than you would have had if you'd ignored it.

But we have some good news: There's a mathematical way to avoid these entrepreneurial traps. In the next few pages, we'll show you exactly how to calculate when the next plateau will hit your company, and what you can do about it.

There are a few basic elements that are the exact same in every single SaaS company ever created. Your product may be unique, but the problems you're facing are anything but. And in our opinion, the success of your company depends on your ability to admit that. But we're not the only ones who think so. Robert Smith, founder and CEO of Vista Equity Partners—one of the largest private equity funds on Earth with over $100 billion[1] in assets under management—famously said it like this:

> **"All software companies taste like chicken. They're selling different products, but 80% of what they do is pretty much the same."**

We've coached thousands of founders through SaaS Academy, and we've got mountains of data backing this up. The vast majority of founders think their business is different, and once they see the math, the vast majority also realize that it isn't. This book is full of stories from SaaS founders who have been through it and came out the other side...victorious. In this book, you'll learn how Chris Ronzio, founder and CEO of Trainual, scaled his company to $165,000 in MRR using a single marketing channel. You'll see how Joe Gaboury, CEO of SimpleConsign, generated $750,000 of additional revenue by fixing his pricing. We could tell you dozens more of these stories...and we will. But first, we're going to prove to you that your SaaS company is just like the rest of them (from a mathematical standpoint, anyway).

A Growth Ceiling is the point at which the number of customers coming in and the number of customers going out equalize—and your company stops growing. Matt hit that point at $18,000 MRR. Some people hit theirs earlier or later, but our data shows that most SaaS companies hit their first Growth Ceiling somewhere between $10,000 MRR and

---

[1] Vista is one of the most successful software PE firms in history, and their company-building playbooks are equally legendary.

$30,000 MRR, and that's the main reason founders first come to SaaS Academy for help—they're working hard, but nothing's moving.

We said earlier that Growth Ceilings are preventable—you can fix them before they happen. And that's true. But to pull that off, you've got to be able to predict it. And to do that, you're going to need four key numbers from your business:

- Current Customers
- New Customers Per Month
- Monthly Churn Rate
- Monthly ARPA (Average Revenue Per Account)

With these four numbers and some simple math, you can plot a graph that shows you when your growth will slow down...and when your company will stop growing entirely. And once you know that you can use the rest of this book to figure out exactly what to do about it. We'll run through an example here, but if you want to use your real numbers instead, head over to softwarebook.com/ceiling to find the calculator that we built for you.

Imagine you're the CEO of a small fintech startup called Centsical, whose four numbers look like this:

- Current Customers   500
- New Customers Per Month   60
- Monthly Churn Rate   10%
- Monthly ARPA $150

From there, we can do some simple math to see that:

- Centsical is doing $75,000 in MRR
  - *500 customers x $150 ARPA = $75,000*
- They're losing ~50 customers per month from churn
  - *500 customers x 10% Churn = 50 Customers*

But to predict when they'll hit their Growth Ceiling, we need to do this math on a timeline:

> **Month One:** In the first month, Centsical will start at 500 customers, lose 50 of them, and add 60. They'll close that first month with 510 customers **(an increase of 10)**, and their MRR will have increased by $1,500.

> **Month Two:** In the second month, they'll start at 510, lose 51, and still add 60—this month they experience an increase **of only 9 customers** and $1,350 in MRR.

> **Month Three:** In the third month, Centsical will start at 519, lose 52, and add 60—the growth is smaller yet again **(only 8 new customers** and $1,200 in MRR).

You can probably see where this is going—they're gaining fewer and fewer customers every month over time until. . . they reach a net increase of 0 customers. To see this visually, here's how it looks on a graph:

Growth Ceiling Chart

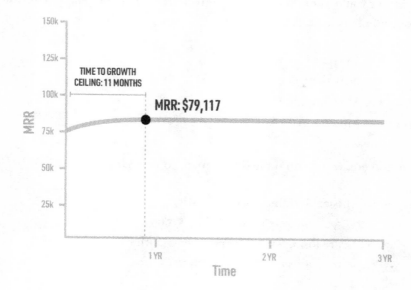

If that sounds scary, we're going to make it scarier: Remember, Centsical as a company is still investing the same amount of cash in customer acquisition, and still adding the same number of customers—60—every month. But since churn *is a percentage* of their customer base, Centsical will eventually hit a plateau, where the percentage that they're losing equalizes with the number that they're gaining—their Growth Ceiling—in just eleven months from today.

When you're at your Growth Ceiling, you mathematically cannot grow.

This isn't hypothetical—like we said, this growth problem is the main reason people reach out to us at SaaS Academy. Until they start experiencing a major problem in growth, entrepreneurs will just keep trying what's always worked—work harder, work faster, work longer.

But then, suddenly, the Growth Ceiling reminds them—painfully—there comes a point when you need new tactics. And if you haven't hit your Growth Ceiling yet, you will.

Why? Because you own a SaaS company, and your company isn't special. Every single SaaS company on planet Earth has the same future: Given a static set of "the four numbers," you've got a predictable Growth Ceiling in your future—a point past which your business will simply fail to grow.

This is not a theory. It's not an opinion. It's just numbers, and numbers don't have feelings.

At its core, your SaaS business is just a highly emotional math problem.

There is a silver lining here. Once you understand the numbers that control your company, you can manipulate them in your favor, overcome the Growth Ceiling, and get back to growing. That's what this entire book is about.

Re-Launching the Business

Matt and Jake had hit their Growth Ceiling without even knowing it. They were spending the same amount of money on customer acquisition. They were doing the same (actually more) work in sales and marketing. And they were still adding customers. But the problem was, the Growth Ceiling had hit them, and they were losing just as many customers as they were gaining.

And for those eighteen long months, they did what any entrepreneur would do—they persevered. They used brute force and willpower. But their brute had lost its force, and their will lost its power a year and a half in. Most normal people would have thrown in the towel—but Matt kept pushing, and eventually came to terms with a universal truth:

His problems were normal, and the answers already existed.

So first, Matt had to swallow his pride and admit that his company wasn't special, and then he had to get back to basics. The answer, oddly, was not to do more. For once, someone was telling him that the answer would be to *do less*. For him, he started by refocusing back on their core customers—gym owners. They actually backtracked on a ton of their marketing initiatives and product features. They niched back down, focused on retention and delivering epic results, and talking to a market that they really understood.

And, while it wasn't "overnight," over the next few months, guess what happened? UpLaunch started growing again.

The ego was definitely taking a hit—Matt and Jake couldn't hide behind the excuses that we all try to use:

My business is different.
My product is complex.
My customers 'don't get it.'

Instead, the proof was in the math: Matt treated the business like it was special for a year and a half, and it didn't grow. Then, he treated it like a math problem, and sure enough—it went up and to the right.

So, Matt leaned in—he learned more about the scientific way to grow a SaaS business—using principles that don't change, no matter what. Marketing tactics that aren't tied to shiny new technology. Business principles that are tailored to SaaS companies but based on best practices that come from every industry on Earth.

We could go into all that Matt learned—and we will in the next few chapters as we unpack our company building playbooks—but the big lesson is this:

> ## Your SaaS company *is* built like a snowflake— unique on the outside, but identical on the inside.

It took Matt and Jake a year and a half of pain to figure this out (but hey, better late than never). That checks out—our data suggests most founders will keep trying to force their way through their first Growth Ceiling for about a year. Eventually, Matt and Jake learned the right order of operations for engineering growth, and the company turned into a success story—they sold for something in the -illions just two short years later.

But why take a year and half of pain to admit that there is a "right" way to do business? If you can figure this out now, you'll be eighteen months ahead of the game.

> ## Your product might be unique.
> ## But your company is not.

***

Armed with this new lens on growth, there are now only two questions that matter:

1.   How far away is your next Growth Ceiling?
2.   What are you going to do about it?

You can answer the first question by using the calculator we built for you at softwarebook.com/ceiling—you can punch in the same four numbers we used earlier, and it'll show you exactly how far away your Growth Ceiling is.

As for the second question...that's what the rest of this book is for. But the big idea is this: There are only three things you can do to grow your company and avoid smashing into your next Growth Ceiling. Not a hundred...not thirty...only three.

And in chapter 2, you'll learn exactly what they are—and how to decide which one to do first.

5 Hot Principles

1.   **You are headed toward a plateau:** Every single business will eventually run into their "Growth Ceiling" given enough time. The only variable is how far away from it you are (mathematically speaking). The businesses that don't plateau are the ones that keep making adjustments before they get there.

2.   **Your business is a math problem:** The way you serve your customers might feel magical and unique, but the mechanics of every SaaS company boil down to an equation. The sooner you

treat your business like a math problem, the sooner you'll start making the best decisions for your company.

3. **Seek out the best practices:** If 80 percent of every SaaS company looks the same, there are a lot of proven strategies you can implement—without reinventing the wheel. Admit to yourself that people have solved most of your problems before, and go learn from them.

4. **You only need four numbers:** To predict exactly when your Growth Ceiling will show up, you need to know:
   - Current Customers
   - New Customers Per Month
   - Monthly Churn Rate
   - Monthly ARPA (Average Revenue Per Account)

5. **More businesses die from indigestion than from starvation:** You don't need to do *everything*; you need to do *the right things* and say no to everything else. There is an order of operations to this game, and you can do the right thing in the wrong order and still lose. More on that in the next chapter.

The Next Right Move

Head over to softwarebook.com/ceiling and fire up the Growth Ceiling Calculator. You'll just need to bring the four numbers we mentioned above, and we'll show you exactly how far away your next plateau is.

Jot down the results in a notebook, or write it here:

My Growth Ceiling is in _____ months at _____ MRR.

CHAPTER 2

The Only Three Levers You Can Pull

"*A business without a path to profit isn't a business, it's a hobby.*"[ii]
JASON FRIED, co-founder and CEO of 37Signals and author of
New York Times bestseller, *Rework*

RIGHT NOW, IN YOUR INBOX, you've probably got a dozen or more messages from business "experts" claiming they know the "one thing" you need to do in order to grow your business.

All day long, content marketers are using content marketing to market to you. Sales experts are selling you their sales tool for your sales team. Playbook pros are offering you their playbooks. Everyone knows how you can execute more efficiently, improve your numbers, acquire more customers, reduce your churn, market to more people, pack your funnel, and gain attention.

But without a strategy, that's all noise.

It's no surprise that all four of us are huge fans of playbooks—collectively, we've built over 300 of them specifically for growing SaaS companies. And those playbooks will drive most of what's in this book: The right tool for the right job, built specifically for SaaS founders. We're talking highly specific playbooks like the Rocket Demo Builder™ (which has been used in the sales process of thousands of companies), the Pricing Triangle (a tried-and-true framework to build a pricing plan that drives revenue growth), and many others. But none of them will make sense or work as effectively as they should until you understand the basic model of every SaaS company. By the end of this chapter, you'll know that model by heart—and then, we'll even encourage you to skip to the portion of the book that you need the most.

But you can't skip this chapter, or you'll never understand why any of our playbooks work, or how to use them most effectively. It's that important.

Selling Software to People Who Don't Own Computers

Johnny's sales guys understood sales. They were so good at sales they were selling software to customers who didn't own computers.

In 2018, Johnny was running Silvertrac Software—a B2B SaaS company that specializes in workforce management for the security industry. Johnny had risen through the ranks as a sales superstar. Starting out as a commission-only contractor, he was making a 35-percent cut of every sale he made—for as long as the customer stayed on board. Pretty quickly, he'd built a name for himself as someone who can land (and keep) customers. His sales chops eventually got him promoted to the head of Customer Success, where he continued to skyrocket their revenue on the back of world-class retention numbers. The company then promoted him all the way to CEO, which is when he hired two of the greatest software salespeople in history. Within a month, these two guys were closing at a company-record high of over 40 percent.

These two reps understood exactly one part of the SaaS business model— conversion. Ninety days into their tenure, "sales" wasn't the only number that had gone through the roof—so had Silvertrac's churn rate: The percentage of customers who had canceled in their first 90 days had increased five-fold, from 10 percent to nearly 50 percent. In other words, Silvertrac was losing half of their new customers before they were even fully activated.

If your SaaS company is losing half of its brand-new customers before their implementation period is over, you've got big problems. For one, your new customers should be the most excited—they're getting the most attention, they're excited about the product, and they should be fired up about the value they're receiving. Second, when that many customers are leaving that frequently, they're clearly unhappy, and unhappy people talk, and when unhappy people talk, your sales team ends up having to answer to more and more objections. Enter problem three: at that rate, you'll churn right through the entire market—and ruin your reputation in the process.

Johnny's been known to say that "everyone wants to be the CEO until it's time to do CEO stuff." This was one of those times—he had to make the tough call. First, he did some research to make sure the problem really was his sales guys. Turns out, they were so focused on demolishing their numbers that they were closing software deals with customers who *didn't even own computers.* So, one day, he and his partner took their two amazing sales reps out to lunch...and fired them both. That afternoon, he physically moved his desk out of his office onto the sales floor and took over the rest of the sales calls, only selling the right customers who could actually benefit from their product. Then, he trained a brand-new sales team (who sat right next to him for the first few months).

As he continued to build the company, he stayed focused on Silvertrac's target market—building their marketing, their sales process, and their product around their customers' needs. With that newfound focus, Silvertrac grew rapidly and garnered big-name attention until Johnny led it through a highly profitable acquisition by Track Force Valiant.

> If your SaaS company is healthy, you've got 3 things happening: customers are coming in, customers are staying, and customers are buying even more from you after the initial sale.

We're Not Building Lemonade Stands Here

Johnny's story perfectly illustrates the three main components of any SaaS company. Every business owner wants more customers. You, me, the guy who owns a lemonade stand. But in SaaS, we *aren't* running lemonade stands. We don't just need to acquire customers and deliver fresh-squeezed juice—we need to keep them paying us, every single month. ("Monthly *recurring* revenue" isn't a very sexy term without the middle *r*-word, is it?)

And there's one final component of every world-class Sass company—EXPANSION. How can we not just keep our current customers, but *make more from each one over time?*

Expansion revenue is particularly interesting, because it unlocks what we call "The Holy Grail of SaaS"—a little something called *Net-Negative Revenue Churn.*

Net-Negative Revenue Churn: Your expansion revenue (from existing customers becoming more valuable) outpaces your churned revenue (from existing customers leaving or downgrading their accounts).

Once you achieve Net-Negative Revenue Churn, even if you never brought on a new customer again, your business would still grow.

This isn't hypothetical. If you'd like a wild example of how powerful this expansion mechanism can be, all you need to do is look at Twilio. Even as a massive company, their expansion has been handily outpacing their contraction and churn—meaning that each dollar they earn becomes more valuable over time. How valuable, you ask?

> ## Twilio's net dollar retention has been between 130% and 140% since their IPO.

This means that every customer account, on average, expands between 30 percent and 40 percent in value per year. And what's more impressive is that they're maintaining this benchmark as they continue to grow—from $1 billion, to $2 billion, to over $3 billion in ARR...it doesn't seem to matter for them. Their accounts just keep growing (in no small part due to their pricing structure—we'll teach you how to do the same thing in chapters 9 and 10).

So, a lemonade stand converts customers. SaaS companies keep them. World-class SaaS companies increase their value over time.

- A lemonade stand has one goal: ACQUSITION.
- A decent SaaS company adds another: RETENTION.
- A world-class SaaS company adds a final one: EXPANSION.

The Three Levers of SaaS

OK, we get it. That's a lot of theory. But here's why it matters. . .

We just defined the only three levers that matter in every SaaS company. And guess what? Those are the same three levers that you need to use in order to avoid your next Growth Ceiling.

Think about it—what we're really trying to do is build a business with the most amount of revenue possible (and one we don't grow to hate! See Dan's book *Buy Back Your Time*[2]).

Your goal is to constantly ensure that the Growth Ceiling can be moved further away. And the only way you can increase your company's growth and increase its revenue potential is by pulling one of these three levers— ACQUSITION, RETENTION, and EXPANSION.

As a recap, here are the only numbers you need to predict and graph exactly when your company will mathematically stop growing:

- **Current Customers**
- **New Customers Per Month (ACQUISITION)**
- **Monthly Churn Rate (RETENTION)**
- **Monthly ARPA (EXPANSION)**

Obviously, you can't change how many customers you had last month, but you can gain more customers for next month, keep them longer by lowering your churn rate, and you can increase the value (the ARPA) of each of your customers. So, technically, that's ACQUSITION, RETENTION, and EXPANSION. Want an easier way of saying it? Get More Customers, Keep Customers Longer, and Make Customers More Valuable over time.

The Three Levers of SaaS:

1. **ACQUSITION**: Get More Customers
2. **RETENTION**: Keep Customers Longer
3. **EXPANSION**: Make Customers More Valuable over time

---

[2] *Buy Back Your Time* is Dan Martell's book on building a business and life you don't grow to hate – check it out at buybackyourtime.com

These are the only three Growth Ceiling inputs that can be changed, and the other nine playbooks we're going to teach you in this book—marketing channels and funnels, sales demo frameworks, user activation, proactive customer success, pricing optimization, and more—they all track back to one of these levers.

And it gets better. If those three levers are too much to remember, just picture a simple hourglass.

Half the Funnel, Half the Story

Einstein once said, "Make things as simple as possible, but no simpler."

And that's where we think "experts" have failed, particularly when it comes to the shape they usually use to describe all businesses—the funnel. Here's the all-too familiar "upside down triangle" that you've seen a million times:

A Traditional Funnel

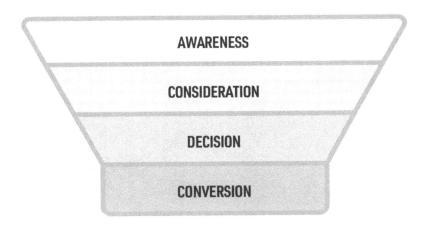

It makes sense. If you're running a car dealership, you need to get the word about your cars and your location (Attention), tell the customer how to think about purchasing cars (Consideration), offer reasons buying from you is superior (Decision) and finally, sell the car (Conversion). And then you dance to the bank, cash that check, and move on. The customer has a car, you've hopefully made some profits, and you move onto the next person. That's essentially the "lemonade stand" model for acquisition we described earlier.

SaaS companies need to do the same thing—but it's only half the story. In SaaS, making the sale is the starting line, not the finish line. Why? Because the other two levers—RETENTION and EXPANSION—are what makes SaaS such an incredible business model. So... what happens to the shape *after* you get to the "bottom" of the funnel in a SaaS company?

Think about the traditional funnel for a minute—there's a good reason that it's big at the top and small at the bottom. When that car dealership first generates attention, not all of it will turn into sales—only a small percentage of it will. In fact, at every step, there's a drop-off—it's completely normal. But in SaaS, we're not supposed to get smaller after the sale—we're supposed to start getting bigger again! Ideally, we aren't still losing a ton of customers. In fact, we're keeping them (RETENTION) and making them more valuable (EXPANSION). So, in reality, the funnel goes the *opposite direction* after the sale—from small to big:

Most Companies vs. SaaS Companies

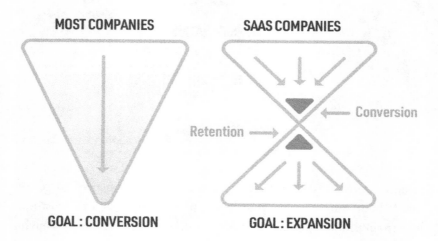

In a SaaS company, the funnel gets smaller as you go through the ACQUISITION stage, and then gets bigger again as you go through the RETENTION and EXPANSION stages—which is why we call it the SaaS Hourglass™.

Ever heard that recurring revenue businesses drive huge valuation multiples? It's true—bottom line. While we can't share specific numbers, we can say both Johnny and Matt's companies sold for between eight- and ten-times revenue. This isn't uncommon in our world—you'll hear from many other SaaS Academy alumni in this book who have had similar exits (Brad from Elevar, Adii Pienaar from Conversio, Jonathan Pototschnik from Service Autopilot, and a ton more).

The reason that SaaS companies command these types of multiples is threefold. First, in a well-run SaaS business, the revenue shows up again and again, every month, for every customer that you bring in (as long as you do your job right and deliver ongoing value). Even better, there's usually a decreasing amount of effort required to retain a customer after they've been around a while.[3] Then, as the company keeps going, a world-class SaaS company gets to that Holy Grail—Net-Negative Revenue Churn, expanding ARPA[4] on customers it already has.

When they're built properly, SaaS companies are money-making machines. It's why investors want them. It's why many of us start them. In the end, there's potential for an insane amount of cash, even in niche B2B SaaS companies, the ones we know and love the most. But you have to start by understanding this hourglass model—or one day, you'll be left scratching your head and wondering why the other guy got a huge exit, and no one will even look at your business.

Nobody knows this better than Kevin McArdle. He and his partners joined forces with Dan in 2023 to create Big Band Software—a holding company that acquires B2B SaaS companies. Kevin has acquired almost

---

[3] We'll tackle the hardest and costliest part – onboarding and activation – in chapter 6.
[4] ARPA: average revenue per account

fifty companies over his career—and evaluated thousands more. He explains it like this:

> No metrics are more important than customer retention and acquisition. Why? We need to know that customers rely on the companies we buy—year in and year out. We also want to know that more growth is possible, and that customers today are still choosing our companies over the other options.

If you want to build a business that's valuable enough to command a huge exit multiple, you've got to understand each of the three levers, because they depend on each other. Then, you've got to know the right moment to pull each one.

The SaaS Hourglass

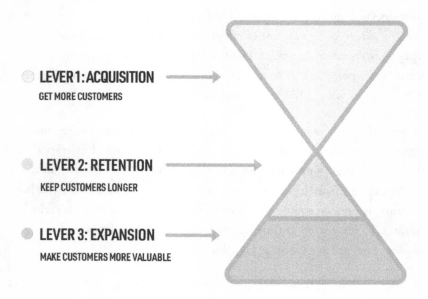

LEVER 1: ACQUISITION
GET MORE CUSTOMERS

LEVER 2: RETENTION
KEEP CUSTOMERS LONGER

LEVER 3: EXPANSION
MAKE CUSTOMERS MORE VALUABLE

In the rest of this book, we're going to go over each of these levers, one at a time. We'll have three chapters per section—for a total of nine more chapters in the book. But in the meantime, here's the high-level overview on how they work:

LEVER I: ACQUISITION—Get More Customers

Lever 1: Acquisition

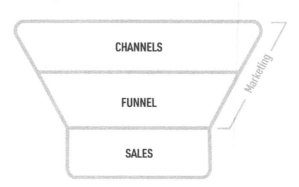

This first section of the Hourglass is all about getting new customers into your world. You start by getting some attention in the marketplace via your marketing channels. After that, you'll capture that demand and move your buyers towards a sales conversation using your marketing funnel. And the last step, of course, is the sale—the point when the buyer finally becomes your customer, and you can start to serve them.

Customer acquisition (i.e. marketing and sales) is interesting because it's the part that most founders think they need to fix, but often, there's other work hiding beneath. It's like climbing a mountain and reaching the top to only to realize that it was a false summit, and you've still got miles to go. That doesn't mean acquisition isn't important—if you can't sell, your company *will* die—it's just that acquisition might not be the *first* thing you need to work on (more on that later).

LEVER 2: RETENTION—Keep Customers Longer

Lever 2: Retention

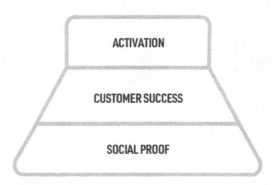

After the sale, your customer first needs to be activated. The initial onboarding sequence to get them to experience the value of your software needs to happen as quickly as possible—and if it doesn't, it's very likely that they leave...and your recurring revenue disappears as quickly as it showed up.

From there, your job is to proactively serve the customer—monitor their usage, ensure that they're getting continued value from the software...and make sure that they know about it. Of course, once they're getting amazing results, you'll need a strategy to turn them into superfans that sing your praises from the digital rooftops (which in turn, will turbocharge your marketing channels).

LEVER 3: EXPANSION—Make Customers More Valuable

Lever 3: Expansion

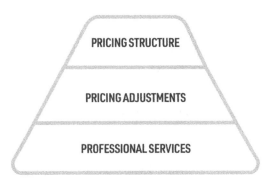

Now that you've gone to the trouble of getting all these new customers, activating them, and making sure that they're getting value from your platform...it's time to ensure you're capturing enough of that value to continue growing the business.

Pricing is a big lever, and it's one that scares a lot of founders—but as your customer continues down the funnel, using more and more of your software and getting more and more results for their business, it's highly likely that they'll need to go through a price adjustment of some sort. It's more than just jacking up prices, though—we'll teach you the right way to build your pricing structure so that your price adjusts organically based on the way your customers are using your software—ensuring that you're making more money when they're getting more value.

It doesn't stop there, though. We're big believers in using professional services to shore up your SaaS platform, drive better results for your customers, and to drive additional profits as well. And if this runs counter to some "wisdom" you've heard before about services, pay close attention when you get to chapter 11, because we'll break it all down for you.

***

If there's one principle that you take from this chapter, make it this one:

Success begins *after* the sale.

Just like the Twilio example we explained earlier, you can see that there's a lot that happens after the initial purchase. RETENTION and EXPANSION are just as important as sales itself, and when all three are dialed in and working in harmony with one another, your business will grow more quickly than you ever thought possible.

The SaaS Hourglass™ model shows how you should think about your entire business. And when done properly, there's a lot more to it than a regular transactional business model (sell things → get money). Yes, the customer journey is a little more complicated. Yes, there's a lot more lurking "after the sale" that needs to be dialed in. But this is what makes recurring revenue companies different from any other business model in the world.

However, there's one more little complication that we need to discuss:

You can do the right things in the wrong order and still lose.

Sequencing = Success

The reason that we care so much about the math and the hourglass funnel is because it doesn't just tell you *what to do*...it tells you *the right order to do it in*.

Remember Centsical, the example company from chapter 1? It was eleven months away from the Growth Ceiling, where it's mathematically impossible to grow.

As a refresher, here are their current "big four" metrics:

1. Current Customers   500
2. New Customers Per Month   60
3. Monthly Churn Rate   10%
4. Monthly ARPA $150

Growth Ceiling Chart

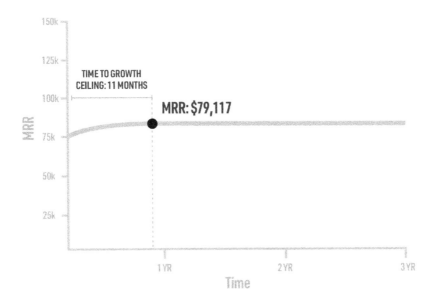

Let's run a few experiments here.

Experiment 1: Improve Sales

Let's say that Centsical focuses on improving sales from 60 new customers per month to 70 (that's a 16 percent increase—not a small achievement).

Here's the updated Growth Ceiling calculation:

Experiment 1: Improved Sales

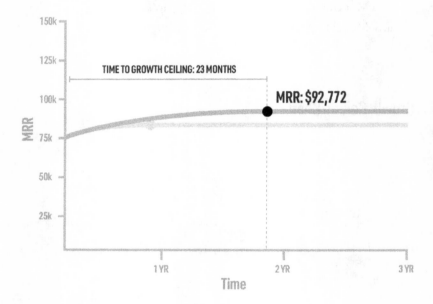

Not too shabby, right? Looks like we bought ourselves a year of growth (ceiling went from eleven months away to twenty-three months away).

Yes, we'll have to invest more in sales and marketing, maybe hire a new salesperson, pay for ads, all that good stuff—but it's definitely buying us some time (literally).

But we're not sold yet...time for another experiment.

Experiment 2: Improve Retention

In this scenario, we'll say that instead of focusing on ramping up sales, Centsical focused on improving retention. For a $150 per month product, 5 percent churn would be a great benchmark—but let's say they just get it to 7 percent instead.

As a reminder, this means that instead of losing 10 percent of their customers every month, they're only losing 7 percent. And they're just selling their usual 60 sales per month—not the 70 we did in Experiment 1.

Here's the updated situation:

Experiment 2: Improved Retention

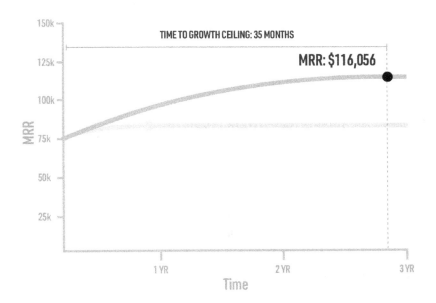

The impact that improving retention has on the overall growth of a company is surprising for a lot of founders. We're working solidly in the "bottom half" of the funnel here—and bought ourselves *twice the runway* vs. improving sales (twenty-four additional months from our Growth Ceiling).

This doesn't even factor in the non-mathematical benefits of improving retention—happier customers, happier teammates, better brand reputation in the market, and most importantly: a higher enterprise value[5].

Yes, you read that right—most acquirers are going to place a higher valuation on a company that's great at retaining revenue vs. one that's churning through a ton of sales—even if they have the same top-line revenue numbers. Ask anyone who has been through due diligence to sell their company (we've done it five times)—revenue retention is a major part of the conversation.

Alright—one more experiment to run here—and it's the one that scares people the most.

Experiment 3: Increase Customer Value

In this scenario, we'll start with the same numbers, but focus on increasing Average Revenue Per Account from $150 to $175.

It's important to understand something here—this doesn't mean you have to simply raise the price at the initial sale. In fact, a well-executed SaaS business model will focus on expanding the value of the customer *after* the initial sale is made (we'll walk through the nuts and bolts of a killer pricing model in chapter 9, not to worry).

You could achieve this relatively modest increase in ARPA by tweaking your plan limits (known as feature fencing), introducing add-on features, services, or a host of other options.

---

[5] Enterprise Value: A measure of a company's total value – and the primary number that drives how much you get paid when you sell it.

Regardless, let's start with the math and see what that increase does for us:

Experiment 3: Increased ARPA

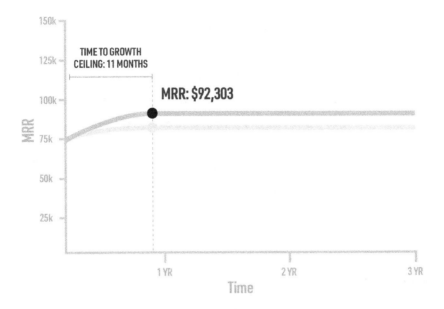

And here, we find out the magic about increasing your customer value—it makes the company more valuable but doesn't move the Growth Ceiling timeline any further away on its own. Think about it—even if your customers are more valuable, if you're still adding and losing the same amount, it won't change your growth trajectory (from a customer count standpoint).

But that doesn't mean it's not important—just ask Tobias Lütke, the CEO and co-founder of Shopify. When Dan and Tobi sat down for an interview on the Escape Velocity podcast[iii] in 2019, Tobi walked through the evolution of Shopify's offer:

> Shopify, in the beginning, was shopping cart software. . . with one major change—we actually made it for entrepreneurs. But by

looking at the pain points of these customers...it has taken us to be in a completely different segment.

Shopify went on to launch a whole host of merchant services—payment processing, point of sale systems, data integrations, and even a logistics operation—all in service of helping their primary customers solve the problems that were restricting their growth. And the result?

> **In 2023, Shopify generated almost 3 times as much revenue[iv] from merchant services as they did from software subscriptions.**

Increasing revenues unlocks a lot for us as SaaS founders—additional investments into the team, into the product, and back into growth. It's the key driver of building a valuable company—and our job is to make sure that you know exactly how to do it.

Stacking Wins

Most up-and-coming companies don't have the resources to do all of this at once—if it were so easy to increase sales by 16 percent while also improving retention by almost a third and increasing customer value at the same time...well, everyone would be doing it already!

In the example we've worked on in this chapter, our assessment as business coaches would be to focus first on fixing retention, and then re-evaluate to make a decision on increasing sales vs. increasing customer value (based on how much we think we could move each needle and how much effort it would take).

But just to display the power of stacking these strategies, let's say that we improve churn (10 percent to 7 percent), and increase customer value ($150 to $175)—and we don't touch sales. Our ceiling is now thirty-five months out with a max revenue of about $135,000. And if we add in the sales ramp? We're now up to almost $157,000 per month.

Not bad for a company that was less than three months from an epic slowdown and projecting a hard ceiling at $80,000 in revenue. The company is now earning twice the revenue and experienced an extra twenty-four months of growth—just from making incremental gains on these three levers.

It's Your Journey (We've Got the Map)

The SaaS Hourglass™ model will guide you through the rest of this book. Each section (and each chapter within) corresponds to a specific point in the Hourglass—which leaves you with a few options.

If you want to start at the top of the funnel and follow it all the way through (just like a customer would)—all you have to do is read on. But if you're more of a rebel, and want to skip ahead, we'll help you do that in a way that makes sense. By following the action steps at the end of this chapter (and using our online calculator), you can plug in your numbers and figure out specifically which section of the book will help grow your business the most—just like we did in the "three experiments" earlier in this chapter.

Each section is designed, on purpose, to stand alone. So (for instance) if you know that improving retention is what's most impactful for your business...you can skip straight to that section and get after it. Same with the other two levers. You're in control.

Why did we write it this way? Simple—because we're here to help you solve problems, not to tell you a story. We don't want you to read this book and feel smart. We want you to read a chapter, implement what you learned (exactly the way we've written it[6]), and build a stronger, bigger, and more durable SaaS company.

You now know exactly how to predict your next plateau. You know the three levers you can pull to break through it. You have a tool (linked below) to figure out which of the three levers you should pull first. And you have a map (the SaaS Hourglass™) to follow along the way.

You're armed and dangerous.

And now, it's time to build.

5 Hot Principles

1. **You only have three levers:** There are only three ways to grow your company—you can Get More Customers, Keep Customers Longer, and Make Customers More Valuable. That's it.

2. **Success begins after the sale:** For a well-built SaaS company, most of the financial opportunity lies in RETENTION and EXPANSION after the sale. You can look to the industry titans as examples of this (Twilio and Shopify were our two examples, but there are tons). Building a large customer base and making them more valuable over time is *the* way to grow your enterprise value.

3. **Memorize the SaaS Hourglass™:** Learn the hourglass model and commit it to memory. It's a great visualization for how your company is supposed to work, and the steps within it are the "building blocks" of your empire.

4. **Sequencing = success:** You can do the right things in the wrong order and still lose. When you're deciding which part of the

---

[6] This is important. Don't change the play before you've run it for the first time. Model, *then* modify.

Hourglass to work on next, run three scenarios and see which one will drive the biggest ROI.

5. **Model, then modify:** Don't change the playbook before you've run the play. The strategies in the rest of this book have been tested with thousands of companies over the years. They *work*—don't add in a bunch of variables unnecessarily.

The Next Right Move

Now that you understand the three levers you can use to break through your Growth Ceiling, head over to softwarebook.com/levers to learn how small and achievable improvements in each metric would affect your growth.

Then, document your findings and next steps here:

My current Growth Ceiling is _____ months at \$_____ MRR.

The growth strategy I'm focused next on is to:

[ ] **Get More Customers** (New Customers Per Month)
[ ] **Keep Customers Longer** (Monthly Churn Percentage)
[ ] **Make Customers More Valuable** (Average Revenue Per Account)

My goal is to improve this metric from _____ to _____ within 90 days.

My Growth Ceiling will then move to _____ months at \$_____ MRR.

LEVER 1

ACQUISITION—*Get More Customers*

CHAPTER 3

The $2 Million Facebook Ad

"Marketing is a game of attention. You have to be able to play the game."[v]
DAVE GERHARDT, CEO of Exit Five and former vice-president of marketing at Drift

"SPEND $3,000 FOR THIRTY DAYS, or don't even bother."

Chris and Jonathan Ronzio's company, Trainual, was making $4,000 a month. Three grand meant 75 percent of their next month's revenue. It was a big ask.

These two brothers founded Trainual—a software platform that helps other businesses quickly develop training and processes—in early 2018. Post-launch, they jumped up to $4,000 MRR through their personal contacts and connections. But as you know, $4,000 doesn't pay the bills when you have a team.

They decided to reach out to a Facebook consultant to figure out if paid ads could be the next logical step to unlock growth. They obviously didn't have the cash to pay the consultant to actually run the ads, so they paid him for his time and advice (and from there, they'd handle all the actual grunt work themselves).

The consultant's first suggestion? Unless they were willing to spend $100 a day for thirty days to run *one ad on one platform*, they shouldn't even bother. Three thousand dollars or bust.

At the time, customers were paying Trainual about a hundred bucks a month, and Chris guesstimated each one would stick around for at least six months. So, if they could just bring on five new customers, they'd break even ($100 per month x 6 months x 5 customers = $3,000, break even for their initial paid-ads investment).

So, their plan was simple—land five new customers in thirty days. They pulled the trigger.

"I knew I just needed to get five," Chris told us later in an interview, with that entrepreneurial, risk-taking sparkle in his eye. "And guess what? In that first month, we got *six*."

Six new customers. Just over the threshold. So, the next month, with a little more cash in the business from their new sales, Chris and his brother invested a little more into ads—$5,000. Same play: one ad, one month, no changes. This month, they had even better results; in addition to the net-new prospects who were converting, they enjoyed a carry-over effect, where some people who'd seen their ads the first month didn't convert, but they converted the second month after continual advertisement. So, dollar for dollar, the second month had even better returns. Chris and Jonathan kept going.

Quickly, they scaled all the way up to $10,000 in monthly ad spend, then to $13,000, and then to $25,000. Every week, they had more revenue coming in, so they spent more on ads, running the same, simple playbook, over and over again.

"That playbook was like a rocket ship. And we rode it as far as it would take us."

If this story sounds too good to be true, it's about to get crazier. We didn't even know the full details until we contacted Chris. . .

Want to take a swing at how far their "rocket ship" took them? On how much revenue that one, simple channel, starting with only one ad, made them?

They didn't add another channel until they reached *$165,000 MRR*.

***

You'll be happy to find out that this chapter *isn't* about ads. It's about finding the right channel and sticking to it. This chapter is going to bust every myth you've ever believed about "diversifying" your channels or needing to work on your "channel mix."

These guys literally took a $50,000-a-year-company to $2 million with Facebook ads only. They had one channel, and they followed a predictable path to achieving a crazy high revenue mark.

In this chapter, we're going to give you our five simple steps to help you decide exactly which channel you need to use. Again, it's not about ads, it's about finding the right channel at the right time and executing on that channel. Let's dig in.

Get To Know Your Growth Engine

There are two critical parts of your company's growth engine:

1. Your marketing channels (plural)
2. Your marketing funnel (singular, usually)

The first thing you need to understand is the difference between the two (and how they work together). Most people use the terms interchangeably, misunderstanding both.

> **Channels and funnels are the foundation of your entire marketing operation.**

- Marketing *channels* generate net-new attention.
- Marketing *funnels* convert (some of) that attention into leads and customers.

Channels Vs. Funnels

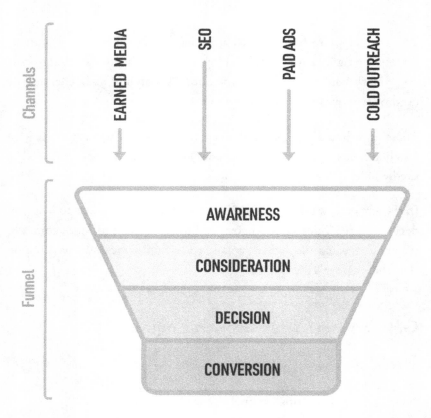

Every company generally has the same marketing *funnel*—the defined path of turning attention into a customer. And every company can choose their own individual marketing *channels*. For some reason, this one concept trips founders up more than almost anything else about marketing—so we're going to get super specific about channels and funnels with some textbook-style definitions:

Marketing *channels* are where you invest time and money to generate attention in return.

There are many channels that you can choose from (which is part of the problem that we'll talk about later). You can run ads, guest on podcasts, write blog posts that are designed to rank on Google, or even take out a billboard over the highway (which we don't recommend). These can generally be broken down into four main types, or "macro channels." This type of classification will help you decide which one to use and how to approach the work. More on that in a minute.

A marketing *funnel* converts the attention into leads and customers.

A well-designed funnel engages with prospects wherever they are in their buyer's journey and helps nurture and educate them until they're ready to become your customer.

You need both of these to work properly in order to build a successful growth engine. If you have a channel that's pulling in tons of attention and a poor marketing funnel, you've wasted that effort. Similarly, your marketing funnel needs inputs—attention—and without that attention, your funnel will sit idle. Most founders invest time and money into only one side of this equation (usually the funnel) and end up frustrated and confused as to why they're not actually getting more customers.

You need both your channels and your funnel working together properly to win. This chapter will be focused on the first part of the equation (finding the right channel for you), and the next chapter will go over your funnel. Getting either one right will help you improve. Getting both right simultaneously will help you crush it. We're going to get super specific, super tactical, and give you our best evaluation tools so you know when things are working and when to turn up the heat. These frameworks, worksheets, and methodologies have never been shared outside of our coaching program before...until now.

Let's begin.

The 4 Channels

Think of a marketing channel as an investment. You're deploying money, time, and effort, and if the investment pays off, you'll get attention in return.

Creating Attention

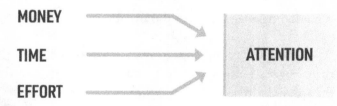

MONEY

TIME   ATTENTION

EFFORT

The thing we hear most often from founders isn't that they don't know what a marketing channel is—**it's that they feel overwhelmed by all of the choices**...and they don't know where to start.

Just look at what's on the menu: Facebook, Instagram, TikTok, Google Ads, SEO, PR, Newsletters, Event Sponsorships, Blogs, Communities...the list goes on forever. Although it may feel like there are endless tactics, platforms, and growth hacks that are all designed to generate attention in the market, the truth is a lot simpler:

> **There are 4 main types of marketing channels to choose from. And you should only focus on one at a time.**

Jason Lemkin from SaaStr says it best: "Once you find a channel that works, lean in like there is no tomorrow."[vii] He goes HARD...even talking about hiring entire teams to focus on a single channel as soon as you figure out that it's working and that it's repeatable.

The four types of channels we mentioned are what we call "macro channels"—which we categorize as Earned Media, SEO, Paid Ads, and Cold Outbound. Within each of these, there may be sub-channels that you can further zoom in on, such as Partnerships (within Earned Media) or Instagram (within Paid Ads). The goal here is to have you focus as tightly as possible (just like Trainual did)—because the more you focus on one channel, the more you'll learn and be able to grow.

Let's rock through the four macro channels to find the right one for your company:

Channel 1: Earned Media and Partnerships

So, remember, the goal of every single channel is to draw attention into the marketing funnel, the same one that every company has. Again—and we can't say it enough—SaaS companies are shaped like an hourglass. ACQUISITION on the top half, leading to a chokepoint at conversion, then RETENTION and EXPANSION on the bottom half. So, in this book, we'll be traveling through the hourglass. And channels sit right at the top of the whole thing.

The first channel we're going to discuss is earned media and partnerships.

Borrowing Attention

The easiest way to think about earned media (or partnerships) is that you're borrowing attention from someone who has already done the work to build an audience.

All earned media strategies are built upon a single question:

"Who are my customers *already* paying attention to?"

From there, the goal of earned media/partnerships is simple: find a way to get your partners talking about you, featuring your platform, or giving you access to *their* audience. And this type of channel can be quite rewarding—it's one of the most cost-effective and quick ways to start building authority in any market.

The most obvious (and oldest) example of earned media is traditional Public Relations and news media (TV, newspapers, magazines, etc.). And yes, getting featured in *Tech Crunch* might feel cool...but in our opinion, these traditional channels aren't the most potent form of earned media anymore (at least not for SaaS).

Modern earned media is all about capitalizing on other people's content—which means that guesting on podcasts, speaking at industry events, collaborating on social media with influential people in your industry, guest-posting on industry blogs, getting featured in industry newsletters, and doing joint webinars with influential people and brands are all high up on the list.

Dan's prior book launch was a great example of using earned media/partnerships- when he was ramping up to release *Buy Back Your Time*, he tripled-down on earned media as a way to generate attention about the book (if you know Dan, you know just doubling-down wasn't enough). In the three months leading up to the release, he was a guest on over a hundred podcasts—sometimes doing as many as six interviews in a single day—all in the spirit of partnering with others who already had the attention of his target audience. Eventually, that strategy built a huge book launch which turned into a sold-out launch event, which then helped that book reach best-seller status on both Amazon and *The Wall Street Journal*.

There's one big risk to this whole earned media channel: not capturing the attention that you're generating and pulling it into your marketing funnel. Earned Media is the only channel that's not pushing people back to a web property that you own. You're on someone else's platform, and you have to proactively build a conduit that moves that attention back to your marketing funnel.

Earned Media Demand Generation

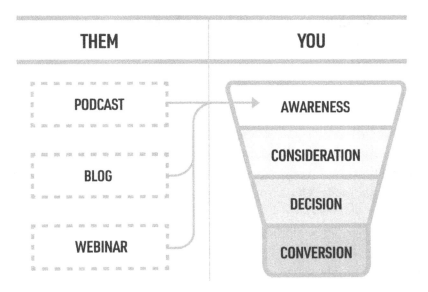

There's one key to ensure that you move attention you created in earned media/partnerships back into your marketing funnel: *the lead magnet.*

> **When you're on someone else's channel, you've got to have something to give away. That's where the lead magnet comes in.**

We'll cover lead magnets more in-depth in the next chapter, but we'll briefly mention the concept here: A lead magnet is something you give away (PDF, workbook, template, etc.) in exchange for someone entering their email address (and sometimes phone number)—the key information you need in order to capture the attention you're creating. Marcel is a master of this strategy: he's generated over $1 million in revenue for his company (Parakeeto) just from being a guest on other people's podcasts. And if you asked him how he did it? His answer would be that he built a killer lead magnet and gave it away, over and over again.

Just to prove a point—remember what Jason Lemkin said about leaning in hard when something's working? Once Marcel realized that podcasts were going to be "his channel," he turned around and started his own podcast, which let him invite people on it who have bigger podcasts, who then invite him to be a guest on theirs...you get the idea.

Earned Media vs. Partnerships

We also put "partnerships" under this umbrella. Technically, they're a little different from traditional earned media, but many of the principles remain the same. Our favorite story about partnerships is from SaaS Academy alumni David Lecko, the CEO of DealMachine. His growth from partners was mind-boggling—from $120,000 in MRR up to $723,000 in MRR—in under a year—just by implementing a partner strategy and focusing on it like a maniac:

> The biggest thing that Dan helped us do was really focus on a single lead generation strategy. I was trying to do paid ads, we had done some partnerships, we had some inbound going on...

But it wasn't until he laser-focused on partners that his growth exploded—so much that he ended up teaching how he did that from a SaaS Academy stage a year later.

The concept is essentially the same as earned media, but instead of capturing attention, in partnerships, companies often go straight to capturing leads, or even sales. There are lots of ways that partnerships can work—product integrations, affiliate and/or reseller agreements, portfolio sales that include your products...and of course, co-marketing efforts like we've already talked about. In David's case, he was able to have his partners sell a co-branded version of his software, in exchange for an ongoing revenue share on what they sold.

No matter how you implement it, the biggest thing to remember is this:

Your mission with earned media and partnerships is to borrow attention from someone else who's already got it.

The 3 Fs of Borrowed Attention

Looking to dive straight into an earned media/partnership channel? Use this quick framework to find out how to best create an earned media/partnership channel that maximizes borrowed attention:

- **Fund:** Who is your best-fit customer *already* buying products and services from?

- **Follow:** Who does your best-fit customer pay attention to? Think about authors, podcasters, blogs, websites, business coaches, influencers, publications, etc.

- **Frequent:** Where does your best-fit customer hang out? (Groups, events, masterminds, user conferences, etc.)

Take out a piece of paper, fire up Google, and write out the three lists above. The result will be a database of all the places that your customers' attention already goes—and from there, your job is to network, deliver value, and create the relationships with the owners of those places so you can get you into those platforms, serve those audiences, and borrow that attention.

Channel 2: Search Engine Optimization (SEO)

Search engine optimization, in its simplest form, is the art of positioning your content so that it's served up when your future customer is searching for answers on the internet. When people have problems, they hit the search engines to find answers—and you want your answer to be the one they find first.

Google is still the number one player in this space (for now), but there are some other important platforms that sometimes people forget are search engines in their own right:

- YouTube (it's the second-largest search engine after Google)
- Reddit
- Quora
- Product Hunt
- Software Review Sites (think G2, Capterra, etc.)

At the time of this book's writing, large language models are also taking the internet by storm (ChatGPT, Claude, Gemini, etc.)—and AI-based search engines such as Perplexity are starting to give Google a run for their money, too. No matter where the searches are happening, there will always be value in authoring the source content—but it only pays off when it gets coupled with a solid SEO strategy.

It all starts with the keywords—because regardless of anything else, a page is only going to show up in the search results if it's related to the topic being searched. It's easy to tumble down the rabbit hole on keyword strategy, research, etc....but if you only remember one thing about it, remember this:

> **Whenever you're writing on the internet, try to include target keywords that your customer would search for. It's free.**

Specifically, you should ensure that your high-value keywords are included on your website homepage and your product pages (at a minimum), along with every blog post you publish and every YouTube video you produce. That's the minimum effective dose, regardless of if you go heavy on SEO as a core marketing channel or not.

A Note on Keywords

As of the writing of this book, there are a lot of things changing in the SEO world. There are a ton of questions:

- How will the algorithms evolve due to AI-generated content?
- Will keywords become less important over time?
- How will keywords be utilized when AI is actually generating the search results?

You get the idea. The timeless strategy in all this is that you should try to "own a few terms." The tactics of how you do that are changing incredibly fast—but the correlation between the words that your customers use to describe their problems and the content you produce is here to stay.

The noisier the internet becomes, the more important quality becomes. The way your customers behave when they're on your page really matters. Are they staying long enough to read? Are they clicking into other articles you've written?

We don't know what the future may bring—but good fundamentals will always serve you well.

A common misconception is that SEO is only for bottom of funnel keywords. In other words, people only write with keywords that someone would search for when they're ready to actually buy your software at the conversion stage of the funnel.

For example, let's say you run a SaaS company that offers time-tracking software...examples of bottom-of-funnel keywords include:

- Time tracking software
- Buy time tracking software
- Best time tracking software

Why are these considered bottom-of-funnel keywords? Because they're solution-oriented words that someone would search for right as they're about to make a purchase. The buyer already knows they have the problem and they're actively searching for a solution and comparing options. This person is ready to buy.

But here's the trouble: in any competitive industry, these bottom-of-funnel keywords are going to be incredibly competitive and hard to rank for without a lot of domain authority (which can take years to build). And even if you do rank for them, the first three to five spots are going to be taken up by ads, pushing you further down the stack.

Often, the bigger opportunity in SEO exists when we move up the funnel to the Consideration and Awareness level content:

The Right Content For The Right Stage

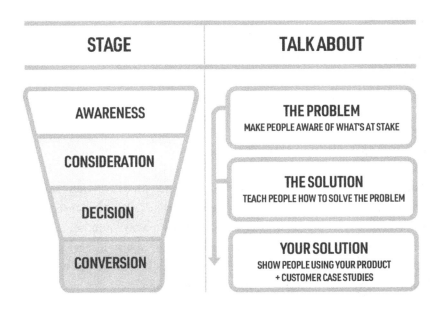

To use the above example, the keywords that competitors probably aren't thinking about that you totally should) are:

- "How to do time tracking"
- "Time-tracking spreadsheet template"
- "How to measure project time"
- "Is time-tracking important?"
- "Which employees should track time?"

The competition for these keywords is lower, which will help you drive more volume. Then (using what you'll learn in chapter 4) you can implement specific strategies within your funnel to convert that attention into sales. Although SEO doesn't usually produce quick results, it can build up to significant amounts of traffic over time—and be incredibly cost-efficient long term. In any case, tapping into the billions of searches that happen on the internet every day, and siphoning off a bit of the attention from that flow can be a great way to build cost-effective traffic to your funnel.

Wade Foster (co-founder and CEO of Zapier) has one of the best examples of programmatic top-of-funnel SEO on the internet. Zapier is a software platform that integrates other software platforms. So, you can imagine that any time someone wants to integrate, say, Google Sheets and Notion...you know what happens next.

Search: "Google Sheets and Notion integration"

And guess what Zapier did? For every single platform they support (thousands at this point), they created a page that talks about integrating it with every *other* platform they support. It's a massive number of pages. But you basically can't search for information about integrating two software platforms without seeing a search result or two from Zapier. They're everywhere. And it's completely by design.

Zapier's SEO Strategy

Zapier
https://zapier.com › apps › google-sheets › integrations ⋮

Connect Google Sheets to Notion

Integrate Google Sheets and Notion in a few minutes. Quickly connect Google Sheets and Notion with over 7000 apps on Zapier, the world's largest automation ...

The bottom line is this:

> **Don't just write about your product. Write about the problem that your customer experiences *before they know they need it.***

How to Kick Ass with Top-of-Funnel SEO Content

We want you to read the rest of the chapter to find the *one channel* for you, but if you're going to rock with SEO right now, and you want a simple hack, it's this:

Create helpful content about the main problem and how to solve it—that doesn't have anything to do with your software.

Why? Because you're not telling them that you've got the best product. You're teaching them how to think about the problem—and that it needs to be solved in a certain way. And (of course) your product should be the best way to create that solution.

> "Your top-of-funnel content must be intellectually divorced from your product, but emotionally wed to it."—Joe Chernov (CMO of Pendo).

Channel 3: Paid Ads

Ads are everywhere these days—and there is no shortage of places where you can spend money to put up an advertisement. Everything from a Facebook newsfeed to the bus stop down the street—ad space can be bought basically everywhere. Paid ads are similar to earned media in the sense that you're leveraging attention that's not yours, only in this case, you're overtly paying for it, which lets you approach it a lot more directly.

The most common place that SaaS companies invest ad dollars is in digital and social media (Meta, LinkedIn, Google Search ads, etc.). But paid ads can extend to anything that involves buying attention with dollars, including sponsorships of events, podcasts, and newsletters, as well as traditional media placements (for instance, ClickUp has billboard ads in most of the major airports in America).

Paid ads have big benefits and big risks. The biggest benefit of paid ads is that when they work, they work fast, and you can scale it up as quickly as you can find the money (think back to Chris's story about Trainual). While some companies like Trainual find their stride quickly and create incredible ROI, it's not easy to do. When they don't work, you're lighting cash on fire, which is bad news if you don't have much of it to begin with. For most companies, it takes a lot of testing and thousands of dollars in ad spend to start seeing consistent and cost-effective results.

If you're a self-funded company, your goal should be to recover all costs associated with getting a new customer in three months or less. The metric you use to calculate this is known as Customer Acquisition Cost (CAC) Payback Period. We'll get more into CAC Payback at the end of this chapter, but here is a high-level example:

CAC Payback Period—A Quick Primer

CAC Payback Period: The amount of time (in months) that it takes to recoup the money you spent to acquire a customer.

For example...

You spend $2,000 to get a customer. Your average deal is $500 per month, and your business has an 80 percent gross margin, which means that you're generating $400 per month in gross profit per customer. You can then divide $2,000 by $400 which equals 5 (the number of months it takes you to earn back your cash).

Your CAC Payback Period is 5 months.

Your goal is to get your money back in 3 months or less.

Even once you hit your CAC Payback goal, staying there is a different game—the more you scale, the less efficient the machine will become, and the more expertise it'll require to remain efficient. And here's the other curveball: you're at the mercy of the algorithm on whichever platform you're running ads on. We've seen it a hundred times with our coaching clients; a company that's been crushing with paid ads all of a sudden has acquisition costs triple overnight because an algorithm changed, a privacy policy got rolled out, or some other factor that they couldn't control. If any of you were running paid ads in 2021, you know exactly what we're talking about. In the third quarter, Apple started pushing their iOS14 upgrade, which blocked a lot of the data that Meta advertisers were depending on to optimize their paid ad strategy. From the second to the third quarter, the average CPM (cost per thousand impressions) rose over 17 percent (from $3.28 to $3.85)[vii]—leaving advertisers scrambling to carve out margins that had disappeared basically overnight.

We love paid ads as a predictable way to scale a SaaS company—- we've used them in all of our own companies—but we rarely recommend them as a first channel for self-funded companies. Of course, there are exceptions (again, see Trainual).

Note: Whenever you DO go down the path of paid advertising, make sure to approach it scientifically and be ready to do a lot of testing. When you run a test, change one variable at a time, measure the change, and keep stacking small wins until you're able to maintain your CAC Payback Period under 90 days and scale up your ad spend.

Channel 4: Cold Outreach

Cold outreach is interrupting your perfect-fit customers—typically via email, direct messages on social media, a phone call, or even old-school direct mail. Otherwise known as outbound prospecting, you're reaching out to leads who you've never talked to before. It might sound old-fashioned or obnoxious, but a cold outreach channel could be an incredibly valuable channel for the right types of companies.

Cold outreach is a great way to get your first few customers if you're cash-strapped, have lots of time, and don't necessarily already have a network. You just have to be willing to grind it out. In fact, Wes Bush (CEO of ProductLed) even went as far to say that most companies under $10,000 in MRR should be doing cold outreach for customer acquisition—even if their strategy is to have a low-touch sales process as they scale—and that's from a guy who has coached hundreds of SaaS companies to sell without human involvement!

If you want to see a great example of this, look no further than Nathan Barry, CEO of Kit. They're an incredible company today—but like most startups, they had humble beginnings. Nathan bootstrapped Kit (formerly known as ConvertKit) and hit his first growth plateau at $1,500 MRR. And he solved it with cold outreach. He niched down, built a list of potential customers, subscribed to their newsletters, interacted with their content...and then sent them a cold email to see what was frustrating them about their email platforms.

It sounds deceivingly simple when you write it on the page. The responses poured in, and he scaled to $15,000 in MRR on that one strategy—which led to an affiliate program that took them to $100,000 in MRR, and the rest is history. And by history, we mean that they've broken $30 million in ARR and have created incredibly happy customers—along with one of the best company cultures in SaaS.

That said, cold outreach isn't just for early-stage acquisition—we know many companies that have crushed the SaaS game using only cold outreach. Andre Cvijovic at Referrizer (who you'll meet later in chapter 7) scaled past $200,000 in MRR using primarily cold outbound phone calls. He has a big market, so he built an army of 100 percent commission outbound dialers (to the tune of 30,000 dials per week), built an innovative incentive plan (where they earned a percentage of MRR for the life of the account), trained them like a maniac, and turned them loose. The end result? One hundred demos per week—and nineteen times top-line revenue growth.

There's just one caveat here—especially with cold phone calls, there's got to be enough "meat on the bone" (aka money) to pay the people that are doing the dialing. Our friend Kyle Vamvouris is one of the best in the world at building successful sales teams at scale, and here's his rule of thumb:

> **Cold outreach is a viable option when your average deal size is at least $5,000 annually.**

This doesn't mean you can't do cold outreach in other cases; it just means that cold outreach might get prohibitively expensive and/or your CAC Payback Period might be super long. As usual, we've done the math for you—so if you want to snag a template to help you figure out if cold outbound is viable for your company, just go to softwarebook.com/channels and grab it.

So, the million-dollar question: does it actually work? The answer, like many answers, is "it depends"—primarily on your market. Some types of buyers respond better to cold outbound than others. But in our eyes, if your price point allows it, it's certainly worth a shot—because you get to learn fast, iterate fast, and take control of the number of deals you're generating. If you can get to a point where cold outbound is giving you repeatable success, it's actually one of the simpler channels to scale up, because it's just a function of adding people to follow the process and work the lists. Just like paid ads, there's high risk because of the capital outlay you generally need to make up-front, but high rewards in that it can scale pretty quickly if you can get good unit economics.

When it comes to the future, however, there is one thing to keep an eye on: AI technologies are starting to saturate these channels, which is making them less effective. Mike Manzi (former vice-president of sales at Workable and Time Doctor) said the same thing when he was on the SaaS Academy podcast—the better that AI gets at impersonating human beings, the tougher it'll be to stand out as everyone floods the world with outbound sales calls and emails. He suspects that cold outreach is at risk of becoming entirely ineffective over the next few years. (Guy Kawasaki even went as far as to say that outbound marketing is for people with "more money than brains"! We're not prophets, and we know that cold outreach can be super effective, but we're just giving you fair warning.)

***

These four categories encompass just about every tactic there is to generate attention. Our ultimate goal in this chapter is narrow your focus by choosing one of them as a starting point, just like Marcel:

In the earliest days, Marcel was scrappy—he got his first ten customers by using cold outbound emails...but it wasn't as easy as it sounds. Marcel personally sent over 300 emails every day...for sixty days...until he was able to pre-sell ten people on his solution for digital agencies.

He could see right out of the gate that cold outbound wasn't going to scale long-term. He certainly couldn't spend all day sending emails now that he had to go build the company, and his price point wasn't high enough to justify standing up a team to do the prospecting for him. Transparently, he was spinning his wheels a bit—until he sent a cold email to a guy by the name of Carl Smith.

"Looking back, it's incredible how naive I was," said Marcel. "Knowing what I know now, I probably wouldn't have bothered emailing Carl...but back then, I had no idea how influential this guy actually was."

Carl runs an organization called Bureau of Digital—a massive community of digital agencies that all come together in a huge Slack channel to share best practices, trade ideas, and generally help each other grow. They also organize tons of agency-specific events throughout the year for agency owners and teams to get together and learn from each other. (Little did Marcel know...Carl's also one of the kindest and most helpful people in the industry).

When Marcel emailed Carl to ask for some feedback on his new product idea, Carl turned around and shared Marcel's info in the Bureau's Slack channel—which resulted in dozens of interested agency owners reaching out to Marcel to learn more about the product.

Light bulb for Marcel: "Instead of reaching out to one customer at a time, why don't I reach out to one person who has access to hundreds of potential customers?"

From then on, Marcel was no longer doing cold outbound as his first marketing channel—he took the learnings he had gained from doing 1:1 cold outreach and used them to lean all the way into earned media. He started his own podcast, which would act as the olive branch to build relationships with influential people in the industry. He started reaching out to the ones who had an existing audience to invite them onto his show.

"Worst case," he shared, "they would share their interview with their audience. Best case, they might invite me onto their platform to speak to their audience, too."

And that's exactly what happened. Over time, Marcel's audience and email list started to grow, and influential people started opening doors and giving Marcel access to their audiences via blog posts, podcast interviews, speaking engagements, and more. Each time he appeared on another platform, his authority would build until eventually, shows started reaching out to him to get him to speak.

These early relationships blossomed into formal partnerships, which drove referrals, webinars, co-marketing opportunities, and most importantly...customers. Not to mention, it also generated tons of free content that would later be used in Parakeeto's funnel to nurture their growing audience (more on that later).

Once the earned media channel was up and running, the next channel that Marcel stacked was SEO. Since he'd been appearing on lots of platforms, he was building lots of organic backlinks (which is half the battle in SEO)—so all that was left to do was take the ideas and content being generated from his earned media efforts and convert it into keyword-optimized blog content. The result? Organic traffic for days, lots more list-building, and tons more customers.

> **Parakeeto earned over $2 million in revenue on these two channels alone—over $1 million from earned, and nearly another million after leaning into SEO.**

Marcel's only regret? Chasing too many other "shiny objects" along the way.

"Looking back, we would have accomplished the $2 million-milestone much faster had I been more focused. We went on a lot of side quests trying different things, when all we needed to do was double down on what was already working for us. That probably cost us a few years."

Another friend of ours, Matt Prados (CEO of Review Wave) did the same exact thing. He leaned super hard into one channel—his weapon of choice was earned media (trade shows)—and he leveraged it to scale his company from $0 to $200,000 in MRR in two and a half years. Listening to Matt talk about trade show marketing is a thing of beauty. He knows that hanging a TV on a wall performs better than putting it on the table. He knows that giving away little trinkets is usually a waste of money. He knows exactly how to pick the event, how to set up the booth, how to capture attention, and how to turn that attention into new deals—because he went DEEP and became an expert. He didn't "dabble" in trade shows...he went all in...and won.

Chris at Trainual. David at DealMachine. Marcel at Parakeeto. Matt at Review Wave. They've all got one thing in common: they used one channel, got it cranking, used it to generate millions in revenue, and only then did they branch out and add more.

Don't worry if you've been hopping from one channel to the next—we'll use all that and call it "experimentation" for this next part.

A Special Note for Venture-Backed Companies

One of the pieces of pushback we get about this idea is that venture-backed companies should pursue multiple channels all at once in the early days. This is true—because they can afford to hire entire teams that have experience in each of these channels from day one.

The difference as a self-funded company, however, is that you're likely resource-constrained—and therefore, need to operate differently. This framework assumes that you are going to be the one spearheading the development of a new channel, and therefore, that you'll have limited time and resources to do so. That's why focusing on building momentum, and capital efficiency in one channel before stacking on the next one is so critical as a bootstrapped, early-stage company.

Go Deep Before You Go Wide

Lasers have a basic premise—they focus a large amount of light onto one point to create absurd amounts of power.

But for some reason, most entrepreneurs don't like acting like lasers. We tend to get impatient (or even bored)—and end up with a little bit of SEO, a little bit of earned media, a few ads on Meta, a couple on LinkedIn, some cold outreach emails. . . and all that firepower becomes diluted.

What if you only did cold outreach, and began sending out 100 or more emails a day to your target audience? Do you think you'd get better at those emails?

What if you only ran ads on Facebook? How much better would your ads perform over time if you really committed?

Let's say you picked one type of partnership, and really leaned in...how much better do you think you would get at pitching to that audience?

What if you decided you were going to go super hard into SEO content, and developed a deep strategy to truly own a few keywords in your space?

You're not doing yourself any favors by writing a blog when you feel like it, reaching out to a few people on LinkedIn whenever it comes to mind, or buying an ad here and there. You need to re-focus all this energy onto the right channel to drive crazy power. Later, just like Marcel, you can stack other channels.

So, which should you pick? If you had to, you could guess. Yes, really. **You can execute well on the "wrong" channel and still grow.** But don't worry—we won't just leave you to your guesswork. We've got an easy exercise to help you figure out exactly which channel you should pick:

Get One Channel Green

You have four "macro channels" to choose from: Earned Media, SEO, Paid Ads, or Cold Outreach.

Like we mentioned, you can *further* specialize within each of these "macro channels." Trainual did this with Paid Ads—they focused almost exclusively on Meta. Marcel did this with Earned Media—his channel was podcasts. Matt Prados did the same thing with trade shows.

The point is, the more focused you are, the more powerful your results. You start with finding the right macro channel, and then you can determine if you need to zoom in even farther.

To determine which of the four macro channels to start with, we built a simple worksheet (which you can grab at softwarebook.com/channels). You'll need that worksheet and three highlighters—a red one, a yellow one, and a green one. This audit worksheet is directly from our SaaS Academy curriculum, and it's been used to evaluate marketing channels for hundreds of SaaS companies over the years.

There are five key questions that we ask to evaluate a marketing channel (listed below). If it's 100 percent good to go, it's green. If it exists but needs work, it's yellow. If it doesn't exist at all (or if it needs a complete rebuild), it's red.

    i.   **Process:** Do I have a process for this channel that's documented, executable, and consistently producing results?

2. **People:** Do I have people dedicated to executing this process *without my direct involvement*?

3. **Scorecard:** Do I have a measurable scorecard for this channel that allows me to measure its inputs (activities) and its outputs (results)?

4. **Testing:** Do I have a testing cadence in place to continually test new strategies to improve or maintain the results of this channel over time?

5. **CAC Payback Period:** Am I recovering my Customer Acquisition Cost in under 90 days?

The Channel Maturity Matrix

	EARNED MEDIA/ PARTNERS	SEO	PAID ADS	COLD OUTREACH
L1	PROCESS	PROCESS	PROCESS	PROCESS
L2	PEOPLE	PEOPLE	PEOPLE	PEOPLE
L3	SCORECARD	SCORECARD	SCORECARD	SCORECARD
L4	TESTING	TESTING	TESTING	TESTING
L5	CAC PAYBACK < 90 DAYS	CAC PAYBACK < 90 DAYS	CAC PAYBACK < 90 DAYS	CAC PAYBACK < 90 DAYS

After you complete the worksheet, there's only one step left: Identifying which one is closest to being "all green."

We want you to focus on the macro channel that is the closest to "all green."

If you're looking at your worksheet and feeling a little insecure about how much red and yellow you're seeing, don't worry. Very few founders have an entirely green column when we run this exercise. In fact, we ran this exercise at an in-person SaaS Academy Intensive and only a handful of companies (out of hundreds) had one column completely green. But most founders did have one that was somewhat close to green—a clear leader—which made the next part easy: Getting that channel "all green" as fast as humanly possible.

We know. . . you probably have "Founder ADHD." If you're like us (and we definitely fit that description), you want to do everything, all at once, right this second.

But remember what the consultant told Chris at Trainual: "One ad for thirty days."

We don't like to put a time limit on this strategy. We want you to focus on one column—which represents one channel—until it's all the way green. Once you get it green (whether that takes a day or a year), you can go on to the next one.

Until then, you aren't allowed to move or do anything but get that column green (the exception would be if you aren't quite seeing CAC payback at ninety days—it's OK to move on as long as it's trending in the right direction).

It's like rolling a snowball down a mountain—it picks up momentum as it rolls. You start with what's easiest, until you can get to a place that makes you feel more confident, then, you move on, building on what you've learned. That's why we say to pick the column that's the clear leader (closest to green), regardless of whether you think it's the "right marketing channel" or not. The goal is to make some quick wins, get the channel optimized so it's *consistently producing results without your direct involvement*—which frees you up to go work on the next one. Another way to think about it is, your momentum won't stop when you get focused on something else.

> ## You'll grow faster by prioritizing speed of execution over perfection.

The other thing to call out up front: sometimes founders feel like the channel that's the "most green" is also the "wrong one" for whatever reason. You shouldn't worry about that either. We're focusing on a channel for a bit of time here, we're not getting married to it forever.

> ## You can absolutely scale a company to over $1 million in ARR built on the "wrong" marketing channel—as long as it's optimized.

So...optimize it.

Some More Details on CAC

As we mentioned earlier, CAC stands for **Customer Acquisition Cost**—the amount of money your company is spending to get a single customer. If you're not sure how to calculate your CAC, here's a simple formula:

CAC = (Marketing Spend + Sales Spend) / # Of New Customers During That Spending Period

Let's say you spent $5,000 on sales and marketing in a month and acquired 5 customers in the same month. Your CAC would be $1,000. Ideally, your CAC Payback Period is under 90 days.

To calculate CAC Payback Period, you'll need to know two other numbers:

1. **Gross Margin:** The amount of money that is left over after you remove your Cost of Goods Sold from your Revenue (as a percentage).
2. **Average Revenue Per Account (ARPA):** The average monthly revenue for each of the new accounts that were sold.

Now that we have those, here's the formula for calculating CAC Payback Period (in months):

CAC Payback Period= CAC / (ARPA * Gross Margin)

So, for example, let's say your CAC was $1,000, your Gross Margin is 80 percent, and your ARPA is $300.

CAC Payback Period = $1,000 / ($300 * 80%)
CAC Payback Period= $1,000 / $240

CAC Payback Period = 4.16 months

We've said this before, but want to reinforce it here:

It's okay to move onto the next channel if your CAC Payback is still over 90 days, as long as everything else is dialed in and CAC Payback is trending downwards on your scorecard.

Why? Because CAC Payback can be higher than you want it due to reasons that aren't related to your marketing channel. If you hire a salesperson and they're not closing a lot of deals because they're new, that'll increase CAC. If your pricing is off and it's affecting your close rate, that'll increase it too. You get the idea—so as long as the first four levels are green, and CAC Payback is yellow, you can still move on (assuming you're not cash constrained).

Growth Stacking

In *The Social Network,* Sean Parker (played by Justin Timberlake), says:

"A million dollars isn't cool. You know what's cool? A *billion* dollars."

We truly believe that your company can get a lot more mileage out of a single, well-optimized marketing channel than you think it can. Each channel helps you move to the next level with greater and greater efficiency. And like we said, there's no time requirement on how long you need to sit with a single channel. As soon as it's green, you've got our blessing to move onto the next one. Colored a whole column green in a day? Amazing. Took you six months? So be it (but hopefully it won't take that long).

The way this works is that your green channels stack on top of each other—and each one will increase your overall throughput faster than the last. Through your work to turn your first channel green, you'll learn a ton about your product, your positioning, your customer, and your business as a whole. It's a big part of why it's wise to prioritize one channel at a time.

> **Every channel you stack will increase your growth faster than the last.**

The other reason that growth stacking works is because each green channel improves your overall market presence, which makes all of the subsequent channels easier.

> **Every new channel will take less effort to mature than the prior one.**

Stacking Your Channels

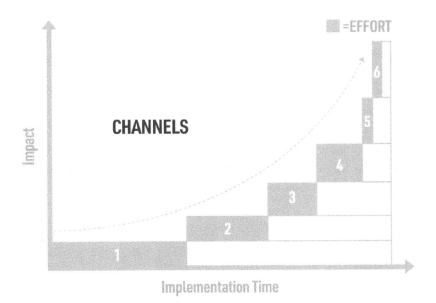

Matt experienced this at his first company, UpLaunch. In the earliest days, they tried to stand up an SEO strategy via blog content, a paid ads strategy (via Facebook), and a partner strategy—all at the same time. Predictably, their blog was boring, their ads were ineffective (and cost him about $10,000), and partner acquisition was moving at a snail's pace. Split focus = bad results.

Once Matt followed the "single channel" approach and decided to focus hard on partners, things changed quickly. Not only did that channel start to deliver rapid growth, but it was the only channel they needed to grow to almost $1 million in ARR.

But that's not even the cool part—a year or so after their first attempt, with a fully green partner channel, Matt stepped back into Facebook ads as the second channel—and it CRUSHED. Why? Two reasons. The first was because their partner strategy was already dialed in, so he and his team could focus all of their "pioneering energy" into standing up the new channel without having to split their focus.

But the second reason was even cooler: because they'd spent the prior year heads-down on partners, a large percentage of their target market had already heard of them. The Facebook ads were just the little push that their prospects needed to step over the line and book a call.

Different channels and different messages resonate with different prospects—it's just human nature. By ruthlessly focusing on one channel at a time and then stacking them on top of each other, you can build a marketing engine that never underperforms and that is incredibly resistant to external influence (like AI hurting cold outreach, or Facebook changing their algorithm).

And that's a fun game to play.

5 Hot Principles

1. **One channel at a time:** Trainual's success story illustrates the power of focusing intensely on a single marketing channel. Rather than spread yourself thin across many different channels, you'll get better results by focusing on one channel at a time.

2. **Understand channels vs funnels:** A company's growth engine consists of two components: marketing channels (where you generate attention) and marketing funnels (where you convert that attention into leads and customers). Both need to work in tandem to drive growth effectively.

3. **Pick one macro channel:** There are four main types of marketing channels: Earned Media and Partnerships, Search Engine Optimization (SEO), Paid Ads, and Cold Outreach. Each

channel has advantages and disadvantages, but all of them can produce repeatable and scalable results. Pick *one* to start with.

4. **Mature each channel before moving on:** Make sure a channel will continue to produce results, without your involvement, before moving on to the next one. You can build maturity starting with process, people, scorecard, testing, and finally, by getting your CAC Payback Period to under 90 days. Get at least the first four of those items "green" before moving on to the next channel.

5. **Stack channels over time:** Once a channel is fully optimized, stack additional channels to build a truly durable marketing engine. Each new channel should build on the success of the previous ones to create scalable growth that compounds over time.

The Next Right Move

Use the Channel Maturity Matrix (softwarebook.com/channels) to take an inventory of the marketing channels you're currently using to attract customers. We've also got a bunch of extra resources on that page, like the Cold Outbound Calculator™, some examples from other SaaS companies, and more.

On the worksheet, just highlight each stage of maturity using a red, yellow, or green highlighter. Next, identify the *one channel* you'll focus on getting "green" across the Process, People, Scorecard, and Testing areas.

The marketing channel I'm focused on next is: _____

The next step in maturing that channel is:

[ ] Process [ ] People [ ] Scorecard [ ] Testing [ ] CAC Payback Period

CHAPTER 4

How To Convert Attention
into Customers

*"The best way to sell something: don't sell anything. Earn the
awareness, respect, and trust of those who might buy."*
RAND FISHKIN, co-founder and CEO of SparkToro and
former founder and CEO of Moz

"IT WAS EARLY 2017 WHEN we started to plateau."

Kyle Racki is the co-founder and CEO of Proposify, a B2B SaaS company
that helps other sales teams write and send beautiful proposals so they
can close more deals.

It had been four years since Proposify was founded, and they'd just hit
one of those all-too familiar points. In Kyle's words, they'd begun "to
plateau." Up until that point, Proposify was a growth machine, driven in
no small part by Kyle's prior business experience (he is a legit serial
entrepreneur with plenty of successes under his belt). But the issue was
he started seeing a "bend in the curve" of their company's growth.
"There's a big difference between being a *startup* founder and being a
scale-up founder."

Maybe you don't feel like you're qualified to be a "scale-up" founder (yet). Doesn't matter—there's a lot to learn from Kyle's story:

Kyle went deep on learning everything he could about scaling SaaS companies. They continued to refine their product and the way it was positioned in the market. They dialed in their operations to build scalable and repeatable processes. They hired more employees (going from twenty in 2017 to sixty in 2018), improved their sales process, and cut down their sales cycle (the amount of time required to close a deal) pretty significantly as well. All impressive achievements.

But here's our favorite stat on how Kyle jump-started Proposify's next season of growth:

"We started creating mid-funnel blog posts, which resulted in a 51 percent lower cost of conversion."

Did you catch that? *Mid-funnel blog posts.*

Sound interesting? I hope so.

Because moves like that are what this chapter is all about.

***

So far, we've discussed the four macro marketing channels. We've delivered the stoplight system so you can figure out which channel you need to get "all the way green." But we're missing one critical part of the whole machine—turning that attention into customers...and revenue.

> **A great funnel is like alchemy—it turns attention into customers, over and over again.**

The well-designed marketing funnel is more than a "buy now" button; it's a multi-stage process that's designed to engage with your future customers at every step of the buyer's journey. It doesn't matter where in the journey they are when they first discover you...when this is done well, they'll always have a way to engage with your brand.

There are four distinct stages to your marketing funnel, and each one illustrates a different step in the buyer's journey and requires a different approach to move the customer down the funnel.

Channels Vs. Funnels

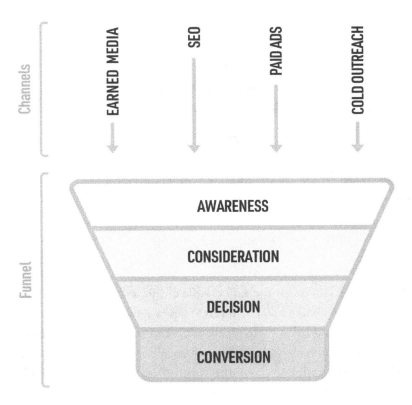

Knowing the distinction between these stages is incredibly important for one specific reason:

> **The attention from your marketing channels will attract people who are at all 4 stages of this funnel.**

Some of the people who see you in the market will already be shopping for solutions, comparing different platforms, and preparing to make a buying decision, and will resonate very well with your "bottom of funnel" content. And although it would be awesome if most of the people who are paying attention to us were at that stage...it's just not that easy:

> **The vast majority of the attention you generate will come from people in the Awareness and Consideration stages of their buyer's journey.**

If you under-invest in the Awareness and Consideration stages of your marketing funnel, you're going to leave a tremendous amount of opportunity on the table, significantly reducing the effectiveness of your marketing engine as a whole (which translates into less sales and a longer CAC Payback Period).

If you want to see a world-class example of this, take a look at our friend Dan Uyemura's company, PushPress. They're a B2B SaaS platform that's specifically designed to help small brick-and-mortar fitness businesses grow. It's pretty niche—they focus maniacally on independently owned and operated businesses, not the huge globo-gym chains like Planet Fitness or Gold's. In these businesses, the decision-makers are usually the gym owners—who are also frequently the head coach, the bookkeeper, the front desk person, the marketing leader, and even the janitor.

Take a second and put yourself in the shoes of that busy gym owner. You've coached three classes today, you're mopping the floor, you're exhausted, and trying to figure out if you're doing enough to grow your business...how many of them do you think are going to set the mop down and immediately decide it's time to change their member billing platform?

Probably not too many.

> ## The amount of people in a market who are "ready to buy right now" is usually under 10%.

So, if the only thing Dan wrote about was his actual software (which would be interesting to people who are making a buying decision) . . . he'd be missing 90 percent of his market opportunity.

Dan, of course, is smarter than that—and if you cruise his company blog (as an example), there are tons of articles around how to grow your gym with social media, how to capture leads, how to get more member reviews, how to build great workout plans...all of which are things that his future customers are thinking about every single day.

This paradigm is what caused marketers to develop the idea of a funnel in the first place. By meeting a customer where they're at and entering the narrative early, it accelerates them towards your solution—and keeps them engaged along the way.

Think about it: how many times have you been watching a YouTube video, reading a blog, or listening to a podcast and learned about a problem that you didn't even know you had? That's top-of-funnel content at work. By design, that thought leader already has your attention (from their content). Maybe you're a casual part of their audience and had no intention of buying anything from them at any point in the future. That's cool—but now, they've made you aware of a problem—and when you think of that problem, you're also thinking about them.

They've made you problem aware.

The next job is to move you into the Consideration stage—and to accomplish this, they might offer you a free resource that promises to help you take the first step to solving the problem (this is the "lead magnet" we mentioned in the last chapter). And once they put that lead magnet in your hands, they've not only taught you about the problem, but encouraged you to take a step forward towards their way of solving it.

In these cases, you're likely either subscribing to their content or entering your email address in exchange for this resource—which means you've officially become a part of their audience. By really nailing the content game in the Awareness and Consideration stages, you're building an incredibly valuable asset in the form of subscribers that can be "farmed" for years to come.

It's one of the most consistent pieces of marketing advice you'll find:

> "The money is in the list."—Jeff Walker (New York Times bestselling author and founder of Product Launch Formula)
>
> "If you're not building a list, you're making a HUGE mistake."—Derek Halpern (co-founder of Truvani)
>
> "It's not how many people are on your list, but what you do with them."—Joel Gascoigne (CEO of Buffer)

As you continue to nurture this audience over time, they'll associate your company with the problem that they have (and that you solve)—and you'll be top of mind as they finally decide it's time to solve it, start comparing solutions, and make their buying decision.

Sounds a lot better than waiting around for the 90 percent who aren't ready to buy to figure it out on their own, right?

> **Your funnel's job is to help your prospects realize they have a problem that your product can solve—and to be there for them when they're ready for the solution.**

Now that we've walked through how this works at a high level, it's time to unpack each stage of the buyer's journey and how to approach them.

The 4 Stages of the Marketing Funnel

Stage 1: Awareness

In this first stage of the funnel, your ideal customer is becoming aware of a problem that they will eventually need to solve.

Marcel has a funny story about this:

> I recently went through this situation myself. I went to pay a visit to my good friend Max, and he took me into his basement for a tour of his incredible hydroponic garden.
>
> He was growing delicious, fresh, green lettuce in his basement. We had a salad later that night, and it was fantastic. As we ate that salad, I found myself in the Awareness stage—thinking about how it's really cold here in Canada, and in the winter, it can be very difficult to find good quality fresh herbs and produce. I want this. I want a hydroponic garden in my basement because it solves this problem for me.
>
> Of course, I barely knew the first thing about hydroponics. I knew just enough to know how confusing the whole space is. There are all sorts of different hydroponic systems, grow lights, power sources, ways of moving water through the nutrients to feed the plants.

There was so much to learn, and I wasn't remotely equipped to even think about how to make a decision, which kept me in the Consideration stage of the journey.

The key to nailing the Awareness stage of the funnel lies in high-value, free content. But not just any content—there's a specific approach to this that we call *customer hot buttons*.

Key Tactic: Mapping Your Customer's Hot Buttons

The big idea here is that you need to get to know your ideal customer at an emotional level. Not just their wants, but their aspirations. Not simply listing out their frustrations, but truly knowing their deepest fears.

What are the things that keep them up at night? What are the words they'll punch into Google when their problem is living rent-free in their brain? You've got to have some solid answers to these questions—and if you don't, you should talk to as many people in your market as you possibly can...until you do.

> **If you can describe your customers' problems better than they can...you win.**

Your goal here is to consolidate your customer's biggest issues down to a list of up to five "hot buttons"—and you can use that list to drive your entire top-of-funnel content strategy. The majority of the content you produce needs to "roll up" to one of these hot-button issues—and this is true regardless of the platform you're posting on (blog, social media, YouTube, podcasts, etc.).

Example of Hot-Button Issues

In Matt's first company, his perfect-fit customer was a small, independent gym owner. The hot-button issues that these gym owners had were:

- Not having enough members in the gym
- Not having time to market the gym to find new members
- Not knowing how to keep members engaged and activated
- Not having time to learn new software tools and marketing strategies
- Not making enough money to earn a sustainable living

Based on these issues, most of his content was based around client acquisition strategies, social media marketing (even though they didn't offer that as a service), and client retention.

The best content in the Awareness stage will get your customer to think, OK—I need to solve this—but what should I do next? And just like that, you'll move them into the next stage of the funnel.

The Accelerant: Retargeting Ads

For each funnel stage, we're going to give you a secret weapon called an *accelerant*. It's one specific tactic that you should employ to help move people down to the next stage of the funnel faster.

> **For getting people from Awareness to Consideration, retargeting ads are your best friend.**

And yes, this applies to you even if you aren't using paid ads as a primary marketing channel—we consider retargeting ads to be table-stakes for any company that's taking their funnel seriously.

Retargeting ads work by placing a "pixel" from an ad platform (Meta, Google, etc.) on your content—which essentially "tags" users who visit that content, adds them to an advertising audience, and allows you to place ads in front of them on social media or in their search results. Retargeting ads will keep your company top of mind, lead the prospects back to your content and resources, and are incredibly efficient to run from a financial standpoint because you're only serving them to people who have already interacted with you.

Retargeting campaigns can often be run for a few dollars per day and still be effective. Dev Basu, the CEO of Powered by Search (which is one of the top B2B SaaS marketing agencies in the world), calls it out like this:

> In SaaS, roughly 97 percent of your initial website traffic is going to leave and never come back on their own. Retargeting ads are the best way to take that 97 percent of traffic and turn it back into trials and demos.

What do you put in these ads? Great question—you're about to find out.

Stage 2: Consideration

At the Consideration stage, your prospects are starting to develop a mental model for how to think about the problem—and in turn, how to think about the solution.

If you're smart, you're going to want to be the person who builds the model.

There are still a lot of unknowns here. Your ideal customer might not know how to purchase a solution, who the players are, or what to do next.

They're probably still learning—watching YouTube videos, downloading guides, attending webinars, and piecing things together on their own.

We can't say this loud enough: there are SO MANY CUSTOMERS in every market who get stuck at this stage. What you do (and don't do) in this stage of the funnel is absolutely critical.

> **Your job is not to convince these prospects to buy. Your job is to teach them how to think.**

Key Tactic: Lead Magnets

A lead magnet is a gated piece of content—something that's more valuable, actionable, and useful than your free content—that a prospect would be willing to enter their email address (and sometimes their phone number) in order to receive it for free.

When you're thinking about lead magnets, nobody knows better than our friend Taki Moore, who says that lead magnets should be S.A.G.E.— *Short, Actionable, Goal-oriented, and Easy to implement.* Founders tend to overbuild these—and it's completely unnecessary. That massive eighty-six-page "whitepaper" will likely drive less revenue than a quick PDF teaching a framework or tactic—because it's all information and no action. If you want a template for building a world-class lead magnet, head to softwarebook.com/funnel and snag ours—it's the same format we've used in our own companies.

But here's the 4-D Chess move: a world-class lead magnet not only teaches your customer how to think about their problem...**it teaches them to think about it in such a way that it positions your platform as the only viable solution.**

And that open loop we left you about your retargeting ads? Yeah...lead magnets are the answer.

> **When someone consumes your content and leaves, serve them a retargeting ad with a lead magnet—like clockwork.**

Your lead magnet should be related to the same "hot button issue" that the content was about—but if you only have one, don't let this stop you. Proactively putting the lead magnet in front of a prospect will make them much more likely to start figuring out how to solve the problem—which is exactly what you should be teaching them.

Remember Matt's example earlier about gym owners? Their top "hot button issue" was needing more members, so, UpLaunch's first lead magnet taught customers exactly how to market their gyms to their past members using a few simple email templates. This lead magnet taught UpLaunch's customers the importance of email marketing, showed them exactly how to do it, and (of course) was also a strategy that his software could put on autopilot. That one lead magnet generated over $500,000 in sales for his company, because it aligned directly to their customers' most painful "hot button."

The Accelerant: Email and Phone Nurture Sequences

Alright, so you've got a prospect who downloaded your lead magnet—they're interested in figuring out how to solve a problem, and they've grabbed a resource from you that teaches them how to do it.

Now what the heck do you do?

Dan always says, "the fortune is in the follow up"—and this strategy is a perfect example. But first, let's make sure you don't make a (very common) rookie mistake:

> **Don't deliver your lead magnet directly in the browser after an opt-in. The prospect should put their email address in, and you should then email them a link to the lead magnet.**

Why? Two reasons. First off, you miss the opportunity to put a well-designed "thank you" page in front of them—which is a HUGE missed opportunity that costs founders a ton of sales calls. A subset of people who download the lead magnet are ready for a sales conversation right now, and your thank you page should give them an opportunity to schedule one directly. And the second reason? If you take them right to the lead magnet in the browser, they can put in a fake email address and still get the download—defeating the entire purpose of getting their information in the first place.

If the fortune truly IS in the follow up, make sure you can actually follow up—and part of that is doing everything you can to capture real contact information from your prospects.

But delivering the lead magnet itself is just the tip of the iceberg. This delivery email should kick off a sequence of outreach where you can **continue to offer additional help—in context of what they downloaded.**

For instance, if they downloaded a lead magnet about pricing optimization, your follow up email sequence might include:

- An offer to jump on a call and help them assess their current pricing
- A case study about a customer who changed their pricing and doubled revenue
- Tips and tricks for executing a price increase properly

If your deal size is large enough, you can also pick up the phone and call these prospects to offer help on the topic they're interested in. Either way, the idea is simple:

> **Once someone downloads a lead magnet, you should view it as the beginning of a conversation.**

And if you run the conversation from a place of service (instead of from a place of selling), you'll build additional goodwill with your prospects—and get a whole bunch of them to keep moving down the funnel without pissing them off.

Stage 3: Decision

The Decision stage is where your potential customer starts to get serious about buying something. They're comparing the available solutions, looking at features, looking at pricing, and determining which platform makes the most sense for them.

And that's exactly what the narrative should be about in this stage: guiding your customer into making the right decision (i.e., choosing you, obviously).

Key Tactic: A World-Class Website

At this stage, your company's marketing website is your best friend. It's something that is easy to neglect in lieu of sexier strategies like paid ads or podcast appearances—but it's still the true foundation of your reputation on the internet, and it deserves some intense focus if you want it to live up to its full potential.

Your website is where sales-ready prospects are going to go to look at the features and benefits of your software. They'll be cruising around, reading your copy, and formulating the most important opinion of all.

> ## When a prospect reads your website, they're deciding whether or not what you've built is "for them."

And the most common mistake that we see founders make? Having weak positioning on the website, specifically around who you serve and how you serve them. When a buyer is ready to make a decision, they're trying to confirm that your software is "for them"—, and your website should clearly and explicitly explain whether or not that's true. Don't leave it up to your prospects...you've got to control the narrative.

Other key elements include super-dialed product and feature pages, some solid case studies that map back to your ideal customer profile, and of course a one-click path to your free trial or demo booking page.

The Accelerant: Everything, All Together

No new whiz-bang tactics are needed here—just some small tweaks. The sum of the parts is what gets the job done—the recipe is a solid combination of retargeting ads (ideally a different set that are driving straight towards the trial or demo), email marketing with a strong call to action, and a continued journey of offering contextual help.

At this point, your prospect has consumed your content, understood your point of view in the market, admitted that they have a problem (that maybe you taught them about), downloaded a lead magnet from you that teaches them how to solve the problem, built a dialogue over email and/or phone conversations with you, and on top of it, they're "seeing your ads everywhere" (i.e., are part of your retargeting audience).

It's a neat place to be—and it's a great illustration of the behind-the-scenes work that it truly takes to make the sales conversation feel easy.

Stage 4: Conversion

Conversion is less of a funnel stage and more of a destination. The customer has gone through this journey and has decided to invest in a product to solve the problem—all that's left is to make sure that they choose yours.

And this one key step is so important that we've dedicated the entire next chapter to it—because the reality is that everything you've ever wanted in your business is on the other side of being able to sell.

> **As a founder, you are a salesperson. You sell a product. You sell a vision. You sell a place to work. You sell a point of view in the market. Every single one of us is "in sales."**

Lots more to come on this in chapter 5—but first things first...just like we did for your marketing channels, it's time to walk through a quick audit process so you know what part of your marketing funnel needs your attention.

Auditing Your Marketing Funnel

Let's make sure we're all on the same page here. We've walked through four key funnel stages:

1. Awareness
2. Consideration
3. Decision
4. Conversion

And for each stage, there's a key tactic that's been identified:

1. Awareness: **Content**
2. Consideration: **Lead Magnets**
3. Decision: **Marketing Website**
4. Conversion: **Trial or Demo Process**

Last but not least, we talked about an accelerant that should be implemented to move prospects between stages faster:

1. Awareness → Consideration: **Retargeting Ads**
2. Consideration → Decision: **Email and Phone Nurture**
3. Decision → Conversion: **All of The Above**

A strong funnel with sound infrastructure will keep your future customers from leaking out—or from getting stuck along the way. Most likely, as we walked through the stages, key tactics, and accelerants, you might have thought about some areas in your business that need work—or some components that you haven't implemented at all yet.

It's all good—that's why we're doing this work. But in order to optimize your funnel, you first need to find its weak points (just like we did when we audited our marketing channels). We'll use the same traffic light system again, but for all of the components of the funnel itself. If you're nailing the key tactic and the accelerant, that stage should be green. If the key tactic needs work, or you don't have your accelerant installed, it's a yellow. And of course, if you're missing pieces entirely, or it's entirely ineffective, mark it as a red.

The Marketing Funnel Map

STAGE	KEY TACTIC	ACCELERANT
AWARENESS	CONTENT	RETARGETING ADS
CONSIDERATION	LEAD MAGNET	EMAIL & PHONE NURTURE
DECISION	WEBSITE	
CONVERSION	TRIAL/DEMO	ALL OF THE ABOVE

If you want a fillable version of this worksheet, along with some examples and teardowns, head over to softwarebook.com/funnel—you'll find everything you need to complete this exercise for your own business.

Sequencing for Success

When you work through this exercise, your funnel will probably have more yellow (or red) than you'd like. But not to worry—that's to be expected, and the prioritization is pretty easy.

> **All things being equal—you should start fixing your funnel at the bottom and work your way up.**

The reasoning is simple: in everything we do, we want to start as close to our customers as possible and work our way out. If you start fixing your funnel from the top, you might put in a ton of work, move people down, have lots of sales conversations, and realize that the problems you were talking about don't actually translate into paying customers.

And when it comes to being close to your customers, there's literally nothing closer than the exact moment that you ask for the sale. The stakes are high. The lessons come fast. And the payoff is that your business can actually...well, grow.

Nobody knows this better than Alex Duta—a very impressive young founder of a venture backed startup called Albiware who tripled his close rates using the framework you'll learn in the next chapter. Without nailing this one skill, you run the risk of erasing all of your hard work on channels and funnels—so sharpen your pencils.

This next one is gonna be fun.

5 Hot Principles

1. **Meet them where they're at:** In most markets, less than 10 percent of people are actively looking to purchase a solution at any given moment in time. The other 90 percent are either in the Consideration or Awareness stage of the buyer's journey. To maximize your ROI, you must have content in your funnel that engages the 90 percent and helps guide them to a solution.

2. **Teach them about their problems:** Awareness-level content is free and ungated content designed to educate your market about the problems they face in their business. This content should focus on the five hot-button issues that are keeping your ideal customer awake at night.

3. **Teach them how to think:** Once your customer is "problem aware," Consideration-level content should promise them a first step towards a solution. Whether it's a template, model, training video, or guide, the best lead magnets teach your customer how

to think about solving the problem in a way that positions your product as the best solution. Remember to ask for an email or phone number in exchange for a lead magnet.

4.   **Teach them who you are:** The final step in the buyer's journey is the Decision phase. At this point, they're actively looking to solve their problem—and your job is to help them make a decision. This is where a strong website with clear positioning is critically important.

5.   **Remind them what to do next:** Use retargeting ads to get back in front of your website traffic and leads, even if they're not on your website—and point them to the next step in the buyer's journey. Use email marketing and phone calls to offer more help to leads that download your lead magnets in order to move them towards a decision.

The Next Right Move

Head to softwarebook.com/funnel. There, you'll find a ton of free resources, including our Beacon Lead Magnet Builder™, the Funnel Audit Worksheet™, and a bunch of examples on how to build a world-class funnel for your SaaS company.

Next, grab your highlighters and use the Funnel Audit Worksheet™ to assess the health of each stage in your marketing funnel.

- If something is working well—highlight it green.
- If it's working ok or is missing an accelerant—highlight it yellow.
- If it's non-existent or working poorly—highlight it red.

Starting from the bottom of your funnel, identify the first red area. That should be your next focus. If you have no reds, start again from the bottom and work on your first yellow.

The next place I'll improve my funnel is: _____

CHAPTER 5

Shatter the Sales Chokepoint: The Rocket Demo Builder™

"Salespeople who are intelligent and helpful, rather than aggressive and high-pressure, are most successful with today's empowered buyers."[viii]
MARK ROBERGE, author of *The Sales Acceleration Formula*

ALEX DUTA IS THE FOUNDER and CEO of Albi—the world's premier software platform for owners and managers of restoration companies worldwide. And believe me—Alex knows restoration. He comes from the industry; as a teenager, Alex co-founded a restoration business named Romexterra with his father, which they started in their home and grew into an eight-figure business in just a few years. A short while after, now in his mid-twenties, Alex started eyeing his next entrepreneurial venture—a software platform to provide an all-in-one solution for restorers to manage their projects, invoices, vendors, payroll, inventory...basically everything.

A solution like that didn't exist...until Alex built Albiware.

When the company first launched in 2020, Alex handled all the sales calls personally. As a former restorer himself, he was stoked to share his new creation with everyone in the industry.

Sales came, but they weren't coming fast enough to support his growth plan—his close rate was hovering around 15 percent. After Alex joined SaaS Academy, we showed him the same highly-specific sales methodology that's in this chapter—called the Rocket Demo Builder™ – and he realized that sales isn't about reciting a script or pressuring people into doing things.

Sales is about understanding the mindset of your buyer.

"I was always value stacking, value stacking, value stacking." said Alex.

In other words, he was showing every prospect...every feature...every time.

And that was the problem. Alex knew every single dark corner of restoration and had built a platform to solve *everything*. But restorers weren't getting on sales calls to find out how powerful Alex's software is. They were getting on the call to fix *a specific pain point about their business*.

This is where a ton of SaaS founders—particularly the technical founders who built the software—have a hard time. They can't let go. Literally, they won't let you get off the phone until they've told you everything their software can do. Thankfully, Alex *did* let go of his ego. He reoriented his entire sales process around our methodology. He simplified it so much that he only focused on *three* core features of his software (at the most).

Which three features? Glad you asked—because this is where the beauty lies. **He lets the customer decide.** At the beginning of the call, he spends time figuring out exactly what their pain points are, and then shows them exactly how Albiware can solve them. And then he stops showing them features and closes the deal instead.

At first, it was painful for Alex, because in his words, he felt like he was "oversimplifying" his entire software platform. Which to be fair, he was. But the proof was in the metrics:

> **Alex's close rate nearly tripled –from 15% to almost 40%. By doing less.**

He just had to realize a hard truth, that every SaaS founder and salesperson must eventually realize as well:

> **Customers don't care about your product. They care about their pain.**

The Chokepoint: A Clog in the Funnel

A chokepoint is the most important and most vulnerable place in a system—a small tweak can drive massive improvement across the entire operation. There's no better example of this phenomenon than the biggest trade route between Europe and Asia on Earth: the Suez Canal.

For context, about sixty-eight ships travel down the Suez Canal every single day. For a canal that's only about 200 meters wide, it's wild to imagine that over 12 percent of global trade passes through it. A 2021 *Bloomberg* article[7] put it like this:

> Consider every item within ten feet of you right now. Shoes, furniture, toys, pens, phones, computers—if you live in Europe or

---

[7]   https://www.bloomberg.com/news/features/2021-06-24/how-the-billion-dollar-ever-given-cargo-ship-got-stuck-in-the-suez-canal

North America, there's a very good chance they sailed through the Suez Canal.

And in 2021, as one of the largest cargo ships in the world was making this exact journey, a small miscalculation clogged the entire globe. As the *Ever Given* was traveling through this narrow channel, high winds (and bad piloting) managed to throw the barge off course...just a few degrees. But that was enough to get it stuck sideways in the channel—and everything else ground to a halt.

Oops.

Instantly, much of the world's trade stopped, all because of that one ship blocking a critical throughway. Every day the ship remained lodged in the Suez Canal, **$10 billion in global trade was delayed.** Hundreds of ships waited on either side of the waterway, unable to travel to their destinations until the Ever Given was dislodged. You can assume that every American retailer was a little upset.

Like a good old-fashioned clog in the drainpipe, the world's economy slowed because of a small miscalculation.

Can one ship really cause that much damage to the global economy? Absolutely. As long as that ship gets stuck in just the right place—a chokepoint that acts as a gateway to world trade.

Just like the Suez Canal, your sales process is the most critical chokepoint in your business—which is why it sits at the narrowest part of the Hourglass.

Think about it for a minute—if your sales process isn't working, very little else actually matters. You can drive tons of attention with the most dialed marketing channels in the world. Your funnel can be rock solid, with perfect retargeting ads, killer email sequences, and incredible case studies.

> ## Nothing matters if you can't make a sale.
> ## Period.

In this chapter, we're diving straight into the spot where Alex was stuck—right in the middle of the Hourglass...the spot that drives the most value...the point of sale. And just like Alex, we'll help you unclog the spot where so many would-be customers get hung up.

We're going to walk through the exact sales methodology that Alex used—it just works. It's a very specific framework that has been used by all of us (and most of our clients)—with incredibly consistent results.

> ## This framework has been used to sell over a
> ## billion dollars' worth of software.

And now, it's also inside this book that probably cost you less than $20.

Give Demos, Not Tours

We're going to be real here—if you're jumping into a sales call with a shiny slide deck and pre-rehearsed list of the 47 different features that you just need to show someone...**you're doing it wrong.** But so many of us make this exact mistake...day after day...demo after demo...lost deal after lost deal.

Why does this keep happening? It's because we resist the truth:

> ## Nobody cares about what you've built. They
> ## just care about getting their problem solved.

As soon as you admit this, you'll realize that you're not doing a sales call to "show someone your software"—and everything about your sales process will get better. April Dunford (a friend of ours and bestselling author of *Obviously Awesome*[8]) says it best: "A great sales pitch isn't just about the product; it's about the customer's problem and how you uniquely solve it."

When you focus on solving problems instead of demonstrating features, you'll start to know your customers better. You'll start to see patterns in the types of prospects you're talking to, the problems they say they have, and what you need to show them in order to solve those problems. You'll start to develop a playbook. And you'll start to close more deals as a result.

Think about it—if you were out snowboarding and broke your femur, you probably wouldn't ask the paramedic to describe every little tool they had in the ambulance before they gave you some pain medicine. Assuming they're good at their job, they're going to go right to work, giving you an IV and splinting your leg, because they've done this before, and they know exactly what you need.

This is how you should interact with your customers on sales calls. They should feel like you've been there before. They should have confidence that you know how to solve the problem. And you should prove it—fast.

The Builder's Curse

Normally, when we tell a room full of people that they don't have to show off every feature in their software, about half of them give a sigh of relief.

Those aren't the technical founders, though.

The builders...the "Product CEOs" . . . the ones who put in late nights building software, chasing bugs, and writing specs...those are the ones who tense up in their seats. Understandably, they have a hard time

---

[8] April's also just released an incredible new book called *Sales Pitch: How to Craft a Story to Stand Out and Win.*

hearing that customers legitimately don't care about all the features they've built. Technical founders care a LOT about their product. It's an intricate, meticulously hand-crafted 47-sided-Rubik's-cube that the world needs to know about.

This overzealous belief is what we call the Builder's Curse.

It happens to everyone—from artists to accountants. But within SaaS, we predominantly see it in developers and technical founders. It's this insatiable urge to point out "just one more feature" to whoever's willing to listen. We get it—you're excited about your product. But your customer cares about their pain points—not that you just spent three months shipping "dark mode" for your UI or streamlining how your account settings work.

So, if you find yourself showing them the 7th "key module" (that they didn't ask about in the first place). . . you've probably been afflicted with The Builder's Curse—and you're probably giving a tour...not a demo.

Stretching the Gap

If you're nervous about doing a sales call that doesn't show off every single feature you've ever built...it's probably because you're not sure what you're supposed to do instead. Lucky for you, the answer is incredibly simple—and incredibly powerful.

Neil Rackham—the author of SPIN Selling, which is one of the most prolific sales books ever written—says, "Successful people ask a lot more questions during sales calls than do their less successful colleagues."

But there's more to it than just asking questions—you've got to ask the right questions, in the right order, to create tension in the sales call. We call this "stretching the gap"—essentially, you're learning about your prospect's pain points, doubling down, and pushing on them until they're unignorable—at which point you can show them how your software is the only thing that can solve the tension.

The quality of your questions demonstrates your expertise in your market.

As founders (who may be afflicted with the Builder's Curse), we spend a lot of time on the promise (and not nearly enough on the pain). Why? Because it's comfortable. It's not emotionally challenging to talk about how cool your software is. But it's wildly uncomfortable to ask probing questions about something that's already unpleasant for your prospect.

Being able to thrive in that discomfort is what separates the true professionals from everyone else. It's not optional. It's not a "nice to have." Doing this well is the single most important skill you'll need to develop if you want to persuade anybody to do anything.

Every sale happens in the space between the pain and the promise.

And if you stretch the gap wide enough, your prospect will be selling *you*—because the thought of not using your software will feel crazy.

In order to do this well, you need to be legitimately good at listening. Not sitting there nodding your head, thinking of the next thing you're going to say. In order to properly understand the pain points and ask the right follow up questions to stretch the gap, you have to actively listen to what the person is saying.

Good doctors take in all the information—your medical history, your occupation, your description of the pain, X-rays, MRIs, blood tests—then they make a diagnosis. Yes, they've probably seen a case nearly identical to yours. Yes, they likely have assumptions about a treatment plan. They are professionals, after all. But it's not until they've listened carefully and taken in all the data, can they make an accurate diagnosis and plan for treatment.

> **In sales, as in medicine...if you prescribe without diagnosing, it's malpractice.**

Understand the initial pain points. Get curious about them. Ask probing questions about the emotions, the financial impact, the risks to the business...find out everything that's beneath the surface. And only once you've done that work are you properly equipped to talk about your software in a way that'll make sense—and that will lead to a new sale.

Follow the Flow of Energy

Before we get into the nuts and bolts of how the call should run, we've got to talk about this concept of energy management—because without it, you're not going to understand why we do things the way that we do.

It all comes down to engagement (and the fact that most human beings care about their own self-interests above anything else). When you show up and word-vomit about your features for an hour and a half, it feels good to you—and feels horrible to your prospect.

If you've ever been stuck in a call with someone droning on about something, and caught yourself completely zoned out, thinking about how you can bail out, or what you're going to eat for lunch...you know exactly what we're talking about.

Steli Efti (CEO of Close) says quite simply that salespeople need to "humanize the sales process...or perish." In other words, it's got to be about showing them what their life looks like when their problems are solved. It's not about you, your features, or your cool software.

In its simplest form, here's what this means for you and your prospect:

1. When you're talking about the prospect and their business, it's creating energy.

2. When you're talking about you and your software, it's consuming energy.

If this were a bank account, your goal is simply to make tons of deposits—and the minimum number of withdrawals you need in order to get the deal done.

And when you do this right, the energy of the sales call will look something like this:

The Energy Of A Sales Call

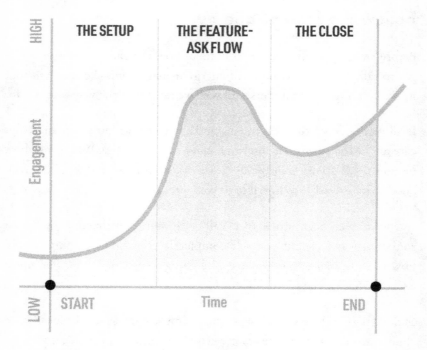

The first third of the call—called **The Setup**—is all about the prospect—you're asking questions, they're talking, you're listening, clarifying, and pushing on the pain. At the end of this first part, they're in the zone, fired up, and very tuned into the problem they need to solve that got them on a call with you.

And the energy is on the rise.

Then, it's time for **The Feature-Ask Flow.** This is where you get to shine—it's your time to show the prospect that you can actually solve their problems. You start showing them some features. They're still riding high, and ideally, they're pumped about the solutions you're showing them. But even along the way, you're asking them specific questions, limiting the features you show them (yes, really), handling objections real time, and re-enrolling them every few minutes.

Their energy has peaked—you probably made a couple of withdrawals, but you didn't tank it all the way to the bottom. When this is done right, you've still got momentum.

And you ride that momentum right into **The Close.**

If this sounds like a roller coaster...well, it is. But for once, it's a roller coaster that you get to design. And in the next few pages, we'll show you exactly how to do it.

The Rocket Demo Builder™ Framework

This exact framework has been directly responsible for more MRR growth than any other framework in SaaS Academy. As we said earlier, all four of us have used it religiously in our own businesses, as have thousands of SaaS founders around the world.

> **Professionals have a process for selling. If you don't have one, your prospect will show you their process for not buying.**

And we're assuming you're here because you want to be a professional—so head over to softwarebook.com/demo to download the Rocket Demo Builder™ worksheet, because you're going to physically use it on every sales call that you do for the rest of your life. Yes, really.

The Rocket Demo Builder

PREP | Research business. Diagnose their problems.	ORCHESTRATE | Appreciate. Check. End Goal. (ACE)	AGENDA| Provide product overview. Review key features.
FEATURE #1 | Address questions? See yourself using it? Impact your business?	FEATURE #2 | Address questions? See yourself using it? Impact your business?	FEATURE #3 | Address questions? See yourself using it? Impact your business?
REVIEW | Summarize key points. Answer questions.	CLOSE| Ready to move forward? Decision makers. Virtual close.	FOLLOW UP | Book a meeting from a meeting.

It's pretty simple: each row on this worksheet represents one section of the sales call (setup, Feature-Ask Flow, and close). And your job is to rock through it, box by box—which will create the energy flow that you need in order to create new customers more efficiently than you've ever done before.

The Setup

Pre-Call Prep

If you flip back to the Energy Flow chart, you'll notice an interesting little detail—the line on the graph actually starts *before* the call. That, like everything else in this book, is by design.

> ## Your sales process starts when the call is *booked*—not when the call *takes place.*

Before the call, your job is to learn as much as you can about the person you're talking to, what their business actually does, the reason(s) they reached out for the demo, and how you might be able to help them.

This isn't some high-level stuff like finding out where they live so you can ask them about the weather. To do this properly, it means some actual legwork:

- Researching them on LinkedIn
- Cruising their personal social profiles
- Reading their company website, blog, and reviews

The output of this work should be a short bullet list of details for you to reference before the call.

Example:

RESEARCH: James McAllister

- *Founder / CEO of Centsical, in business 8 years*
- *Lives in Boise, Idaho—married w/ kids*
- *42 team members, raised $14 million Series A two years ago*

> • *Pain Points: Global workforce compliance issues / payroll tax in multiple countries. Wants to reduce HR spend and consolidate tech stack. Worried about legal liability.*

Pro Tip: Once you (or an assistant) do this research, create a separate calendar invite at the same time as the sales call—but one that's just for you. Add in the 4-5 bullet points that you need to know in order to quickly build the context you need, and you'll always know just where it is.

Orchestrate the Opening

Alright, so you made it to the call—let's talk about how NOT to open it. Over the years, there's been a ton of advice about "building rapport" with your prospect. And yes, it's important to try and create a relationship—but the right way to do it isn't to ask useless questions about the weather (which accomplishes precisely nothing).

We've audited over a thousand sales calls across our companies and coaching clients, and it's incredible how much time people will spend talking about the weather, sports, their pets...ANYTHING other than whether or not your software can help the prospect get the outcome they need.

> **Your prospects don't want to talk about sports. They want to know that you did the work.**

Amateurs will spend fifteen or twenty minutes talking about useless topics because they're scared to actually get into the software discussion—which means they probably lack true belief in whether or not they can help the person solve the problem in the first place.

The first person who needs to be sold is the person doing the selling.

So, if we're not "building useless rapport," what are we doing?

Open the call by walking through the information you put together beforehand—specifically to accomplish three distinct goals (you can use our acronym "ACE" if that helps):

1. **Appreciate:** Let them know you value their time, and lead with information about them and their company (instead of asking them for it)

2. **Check:** Confirm the information you have about the pain points and reason for the call—confirm what you've learned but make no assumptions. Ask them explicitly if it's accurate and if there's anything they want to add.

3. **End Goal:** Reinforce that the goal of the call is for you to learn about their business, assess whether or not you can help them, and if it's a fit, to discuss how to move forward.

The "check" is a great opportunity for you to stretch the gap—when you confirm the pain point, double down and ask a question or three about how it makes them feel, what impacts it's having in the business, what revenue or profits they're not capturing because of it, etc.—they shouldn't be able to surface a single pain point without you asking a follow-on question to understand the impact it's having on their business...and their life.

This is the exact opposite of what salespeople with "commission breath" do. You know who we're talking about—people who are so excited to make the sale that they just start "saying their lines," bulldozing the conversation, and trying to create a high-pressure situation and exert dominance over the prospect.

That ain't it, folks.

> **Your opener should make the prospect feel like this is the only call that you have today—and that you've spent the whole morning preparing for it.**

By opening the call with a short exchange that shows the prospect that you're well-researched, prepared, not stressed or short on time, and already dialed in on what their company does and what they need to improve, you've set an incredible frame.

> **You're selling from your heels, stretching the gap, and positioning from a place of service—which means you're halfway to victory before you've opened a single browser tab.**

Set the Agenda

Once the frame is set, the context is built, and the intent of the call is confirmed, the last part of The Setup is to set a clear agenda for the call. We typically teach a talk track such as this:

> My goal here is to walk through how our product can help you solve the problems we just talked about. By the end of the call today, we'll get you in a position where you can make a decision to move forward.

You'll notice a few things here. We didn't add "or not" at the end. We don't talk about how they're not going to make a decision, or how they're not going to move forward. Sounds silly to write it out, but if you watch recordings of your sales calls, there's a good chance that language like this has crept in.

> ## You need to seed decision that you want the prospect to make.

In other words, explain decisively what we're going to do, why we're going to do it, and where we're going to end up—together, on the call, as a team.

Once that's done, wrap up The Setup with a fast overview of the company—who you are, what the company and product does—ideally two to three sentences max. This is not a tour of the features you've built...because there's a very specific way you should show them off— which we're about to unpack for you in the next section.

The Feature-Ask Flow

Repeat after me: "I only need to show my three best features in order to close a deal."

Seriously. In 99 percent of cases, this is what it takes to move a deal forward.

"But how can that be true? What about all the great stuff we built? What about all the REST of our features? What if they don't know everything our software can do?"

The magic has already been done. If you've run The Setup properly, there's some emotion in the call right now. You've gone deep on the impact of their pain points, the gap has been stretched to the max, and they're ready for some relief.

This is your moment to show them that your software can rescue them. And if your next move is to pull up some goofy feature that doesn't fix the problems you just pushed on...you'll waste a perfect opportunity to lead them to the promised land.

This demo strategy was originally taught to Dan by our good friend Jacco van der Kooij, founder of Winning By Design. Jacco has one of the best revenue minds in SaaS. Founders are usually blown away when they hear his methods for the first time, because they've never considered the possibility that they are more likely to close a deal by showing less of the software they've built.

Here's how it works:

Pick the first pain point from the list and show the prospect the one key feature in your platform that solves it. That's the "feature" part. Once you've done that for the first feature, transition right into the "ask," which is made up of three key questions:

1. Does what I just showed you solve the problem you have?
2. What do you think the impact on your business would be if you implemented this?
3. Is this something that you can see you and your team using?

The Feature-Ask Loop

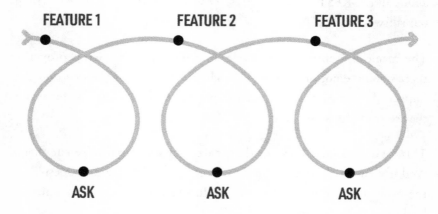

Ask these questions with a sense of purpose and curiosity—and be quiet in between each one to let the prospect actually respond.

> **Silence is the most powerful tool a salesperson has—and a good question is what makes the space for silence.**

Your goal with these questions is to surface key objections along the way. If you've ever done a sales call that you thought was going great until you tried to close the deal, and then you ended up with fifteen reasons why it wouldn't work...you know the pain we're trying to avoid here.

By surfacing objections as you go, you have a great opportunity to resolve them, tie the feature back to solving the pain point that the prospect told you about, and set yourself up for a smooth landing when you go to get the deal done...which is what's up next.

What If My Sales Motion Is Different?

Let's say you're a low-priced offering that sells using a product-led growth strategy. Or maybe you're the opposite—a high-ticket enterprise solution selling six-figure deals. The fundamentals of this process are still the same. The only thing that changes is the sales activity itself. For instance, in product-led growth, you'll need to solve customers' problems inside the software—so instead of teaching them what it would look like, they'll need to experience it. And for enterprise sales, you might just need to run the Feature-Ask Flow a few more times, showing additional solutions for various stakeholders across multiple sales calls.

Here's the part that doesn't change, in nearly any case: You want to zoom-in on your customers' pain points, showing them what the world looks like after you make that pain go away.

The Close

After you've gone through the Feature-Ask Flow, ideally your prospect is pretty fired up. You've stretched the gap on their pain, quickly shown them how your software is the perfect tool to fix it, and they've validated that by confirming that not only would it work, but that it would materially impact their business AND that they can see themselves using it.

There's only one thing left to do...and it's the part that founders resist the most.

Ask for the Deal

Yeah, you heard that right—the deal isn't going to close itself. And for most of you, it means that you're physically asking the prospect for a credit card. If you're in enterprise sales, it might be a paid Proof of Concept instead, but either way the principle is the same:

> ## Ask the prospect to move forward. Out loud. On the call.

So many people suffer from a lack of belief, and it shows up right here- in the moment of truth. I've literally watched founders on sales calls get to this point...the prospect is PUMPED and ready to buy...and the founder says something like "alright, sounds good, I'll send you a follow up email with some next steps—looking forward to hopefully working together!"

Sigh.

Erik Huberman said in his book *The Hawke Method* that "time kills all deals"—and we obviously agree. Your goal is to move every deal forward on the spot—which means that for qualified prospects, you should be making the ask 100 percent of the time.

If it's a credit card, do it in real time—on the phone whenever possible. Dan's famous for this—he'll wait on the phone for someone to pull over in their car and take out their credit card before he gives up and sends a follow up email. But it's the right move. Every drop-off point is another chance for someone to lose motivation and bail out...which is why the best salespeople in the world eliminate as many drop-off points as possible.

"But what if I don't have the actual decision-maker on the phone?"

That'll happen, especially in larger deals. Enter: The Virtual Close.

The Virtual Close is a dry run of what the buying process will look like. It's simple—just ask the person on your demo to walk you through how they think the purchase would work.

Common questions for a virtual close include:

- Who would be the other people involved in making this decision?
- What do you think is important to them?
- How did the process work when you purchased software similar to ours in the past?

And in any situation, if you don't leave this call with a credit card and a new customer...you run the final step, called a BAMFAM.

BAMFAM

What the heck is BAMFAM? Well, it stands for **Book a Meeting from a Meeting**—and in our world, it's the only possible outcome for a qualified sales conversation other than getting a new customer.

| Hanging up a sales call without the next call booked is a cardinal sin. |

And the beauty of BAMFAM is that it works for basically any situation:

- Prospect isn't ready and you can't pull the deal forward? BAMFAM so you have the next touch point locked in on the calendar.

- Missing a key decision-maker? BAMFAM and invite them to the call.

- Need to get board approval? Awesome—ask when the board meeting is and BAMFAM a couple of days afterwards.

You get the idea—whatever the issue is, get a timeline on it and get the next call locked in—before you hang up. Why? Because it keeps the deal moving forward—and like Aaron Ross said in *Predictable Revenue*: "There is ALWAYS a way to move forward, even without money."

Pro Tip: Most people have recurring schedule cadences...so if you're meeting with them at 4 p.m. on a Tuesday, there's a good chance they're also open at 4 p.m. on Tuesday the following week—and that should be the first time slot you offer up.

It's Simple (But Not Easy)

We've talked a lot about "levers" in this book—and how **Getting More Customers** is one of the three levers that you can pull in order to break through the Growth Ceiling and increase your MRR. And yes, if you want to scale your revenue in any significant way, you're going to have to figure out all three of the elements: building out your marketing channels, optimizing a great funnel, and delivering a lights-out demo that will have people throwing their credit cards at you.

But understand this: the point of sale is a true chokepoint. Just like the Suez Canal, a miscalculation in your demo process will bring the entire revenue operation to a grinding halt—even if you have the best channels and funnels in the world.

And after learning this framework, you'll see that there's no magic to it. It's not about doing more, or using fancy tools, or buying some expensive technology. Being great at sales has everything to do with understanding what drives human beings to action. It has to do with acknowledging that everyone has their own self interests at heart, and they will run to you if you can truly solve their problems and help them achieve their own goals.

Becoming a world-class salesperson is one of the most high-leverage skills that a software founder can build. It can be taught—just like learning a new programming language or running a new meeting format, it's a skill that can be developed.

But here's the truth about scaling a SaaS company:

> **Once you've got customers rolling in, you're at the starting line—not the finish line.**

Why? Because this steady stream of excited new customers means that you now have a huge responsibility: getting them activated—which is the most important step if you want to actually retain the customers you just acquired and make sure they receive all of the value that you just promised them.

In the next chapter, you'll hear some incredible stories from founders like Brad Redding, who nearly doubled his customer activation rate using the exact framework we're going to give you (and who then went on to sell his company for an undisclosed—but life changing—amount of money).

5 Hot Principles

1. **Stretch the gap:** Your job isn't just to ask about your customers' pain. You need to dig the hole even deeper—so you can then show them the way out. The sale is made in the space between the pain and the promise. Never forget that.

2. **Give demos not tours:** No more ninety-minute-long feature-fest demos where you don't let the prospect get a word in. You're there to solve problems and get the deal done—so stick to the plan.

3. **Run the Feature-Ask Flow:** After every feature you show a prospect, ask these three questions to "lock in the solution" and to proactively surface objections:
    *   Does what I just showed you solve the problem you have?
    *   What do you think the impact on your business would be if you implemented this?
    *   Is this something that you can see you and your team using?

4. **Ask for The Close:** Don't shy away from making the ask at the most important moment! Your job is to help your prospect make a decision, and you're doing them a disservice if you fail to do that simply because it's uncomfortable for you.

5. **Have a repeatable process:** Do your research the same way every time. Preload tabs with commonly used features. Complete the worksheet for every call. Record and review your calls. Figure out what's working and what's not. Professionals have a process that they run every time—and with this chapter, you've now got the foundations of a process, too.

The Next Right Move

Download the Rocket Demo Builder™ worksheet (and a whole list of our sample questions) at softwarebook.com/demo. **Print this out or load it onto an iPad, and physically fill it out on your very next demo call.** And the one after that. And the next 500 after that, too. You won't be able to improve a process if you don't run it consistently—and this is the starting point.

The last bit of prep before you put this in play is to quickly jot down the five most common problems you hear from customers, and the exact feature you'll show them to solve for that:

1. Problem: _____ Feature: _____

2. Problem: _____ Feature: _____

3. Problem: _____ Feature: _____

4. Problem: _____ Feature: _____

5. Problem: _____ Feature: _____

With the worksheet in hand, and this simple list, you're ready to nail your first Rocket Demo!

Speaking of processes...we've also got a template Sales Playbook for you (also at softwarebook.com/demo). It's a great starting point for taking what we've taught you in this chapter, adding in your own company-specific information, and using it to train your team (and maybe yourself, too). **Download the template, make a copy, and fill in your company's information**—because if you don't have a process, the best time to build one is right now.

LEVER II

RETENTION—Keep Customers Longer

CHAPTER 6

Activation Is a Hurdle
Race to First Value

"If our customers aren't successful, neither are we."[ix]
DAVID NEVOGT, co-founder of Hubstaff

IF YOU HAPPEN TO OWN A restaurant, you might already know this (but if you don't, it could change the way you think about customer activation): once a customer visits a restaurant three times, they're 70 percent more likely to keep coming back. Jon Taffer, who is the host of Paramount's *Bar Rescue* and a great thought leader in the hospitality space, shared this little tidbit on #AskGaryVee in 2017.

It hits harder if you invert it:

> **Until a customer has visited 3 times, they're unlikely to return—even if the experience is amazing.**

On the show, Taffer explained his hack for ensuring that a guest comes back at least three times. It starts with giving away coupons for a free first meal—in this case, it was for a free rib dinner. When the customer comes in and redeems the coupon, the server knows that it's their first time visiting—and they drop a bright red napkin at the table.

The napkin signals to the manager that they should stop by at the end of the meal. And what do you think they do? They give the guest a discount coupon for a different meal on their next visit (along with their business card). When they come back to cash in on the second coupon...yep, another red napkin, another visit, and another coupon—for a cheesecake dessert...on their third visit.

The moment that the guest comes back, they're locked in. They're 70 percent more likely to keep coming back than they were after their first visit. For the price of some ribs and a little cheesecake, the restaurant has just gotten as close as they possibly can to creating some MRR in their world (ok, not quite...but you get the idea).

Come for the Ribs, Stay for the Value

If you're reading this chapter, you're probably pretty decent at getting more customers. You've got some attention in the market, your funnel is moving people along the buyer's journey, and you're stretching the gap, asking great questions, and closing deals in the sales process.

When a customer is brand new, they're the most excited they'll ever be about using your software—but they're also the most vulnerable.

> **Your mission is to drive each new user to the "aha moment"—where they use that key feature, see it fix their pain point, and get excited to do more.**

Jon figured out this moment for restaurants—it was the third meal. After the third time a guest sat down, after their last bite of free cheesecake, they were considered "fully activated."

Do you know your "activation moment" with this same level of clarity?

That's the question we'll be exploring in this chapter—because like we've said from the start of this book, the majority of your opportunity lies *after you make the sale*—and it all starts with product activation.

If you don't do this well, things will get bad...fast. A customer will come in, get confused, and churn within a month or two. They likely haven't paid you enough for you to recoup your Customer Acquisition Cost (CAC), which will negatively impact your cash flow. And even worse, the faster you lose customers, the closer you'll be to crashing into the Growth Ceiling...resulting in a growth plateau that'll put all your amazing plans on hold.

Whenever we talk about activation, Dan loves to tell this story about his team at Flowtown:

Flowtown was the company that Dan started after his first successful exit—it was a Twitter automation tool (we're talking 2009 here, when these tools were first getting created). They had a ton of new trials coming in week over week, which felt pretty good...but there was one big problem:

People were signing up for the tool...and then not using it.

Dan knew immediately that those users were one click away from leaving forever.

> **If you're seeing behaviors that confuse you, your next move should be to talk to your customers—NOT to try and explain it on your own.**

And that's exactly what Dan and his team did—they immediately started reaching out to every new user to have a conversation about what was stopping them from scheduling a Tweet. He was expecting something technical—maybe they couldn't get their account integrated properly, or they couldn't figure out how to use the queue, or some other issue with the interface.

But the answer itself was a lot less obvious: They just didn't feel like they had anything to say.

This happens all the time—we end up focusing so much on the mechanics of the product that we don't focus on what the user actually needs, in that moment, in order to get the value we promised them.

And in the case of Flowtown, it means that users were signing up, linking their Twitter account, getting to the step where they actually had to schedule a Tweet...and leaving. No value, no reason to come back to the app, and no reason to be a paying customer.

So, what did Dan and the team do? They preloaded famous motivational quotes from famous people and thought leaders into that step of the activation process—so that even if a user didn't have something original to share, they could still find something they liked and get it scheduled with the click of a button.

Activation went through the roof.

Dan's team knew that the key value moment was when a user scheduled their first Tweet—and they ruthlessly found and eliminated the friction between the initial signup and that value moment. It was their version of the Red Napkin Strategy, and it worked beautifully.

Speaking of Twitter, they had their own version of this issue when they first launched. In the early days, the initial hypothesis was that Twitter would be most valuable as a social networking platform where people could share about their lives (just like Facebook, but with short form text). But as they started to dig into the data around which actions were driving retention and repeat usage patterns, they realized that posting wasn't the biggest reason their early users kept coming back—it was consumption.

Twitter ended up being the easiest place to find news and current events in real time—it was an order of magnitude faster than traditional media, and their users knew it. The team leaned into it, and instead of prompting new users to Tweet, they fed them a list of suggested accounts to follow. And once you had followed those first few accounts, the Twitter algorithm took it from there.

What's the common theme here?

> **User activation can be boiled down to a single moment in time. Find it and get your users there as quickly as possible.**

Hiten Shah, founder of KISSmetrics (and more recently, Nira) once said that "without a single killer core use case, product/market fit is just a dream diluted by features." There's got to be that "one magic moment" that makes your users finally "get it." And it's one of the most powerful moments in the entire lifecycle of your customer.

We encourage founders to track this as a core KPI in the company—we simply call it "First Value." And when you obsess over your user activation, and make sure that your shiny new customers are all hitting that First Value moment quickly and consistently, you'll be well on your way to conquering churn—forever.

And if you don't? It's not pretty. New customers have high expectations. And if they don't get the value that you promised them during the sales conversation, they'll be let down, disappointed, and maybe even angry. People like this are usually gone in under 90 days—which means that your churn will increase, your reputation will take a hit, and it'll eventually make it tougher for you to get new sales in the first place.

Our friend and client Weston Zimmerman conquered this exact issue in his company, SynkedUP (workflow management software for landscapers and lawn care companies). His customers loved the promise of what SynkedUP would do for them but would consistently drop off during the activation process—which was a big reason that he couldn't get their churn under 5 percent monthly. It wasn't until he focused on speeding it up—allowing salespeople to instantly provision accounts on the sales call and automating activation steps in the product—that the short-term churn problem was solved (as of the writing of this book, Weston's monthly churn is consistently under 1 percent—which is world class, especially selling to small businesses).

In the first section of this book, we talked a lot about how a bad sales process will make it impossible to grow, even if your marketing channels and funnel are world-class. User activation has the same level of importance—it's the main chokepoint after the initial sale, and if you can't get this right, it'll render all of your future RETENTION and EXPANSION strategies useless.

A Lesson in Medicine

When Alexander Fleming discovered the world's first antibiotic, penicillin, it was the start of an entire category of drugs that would go on to save millions of lives. However, soon after it was mass-produced, a new problem was discovered: antibiotic-resistant bacteria.

What do you think would have happened if the medical community had turned a blind eye to these problems and just continued prescribing penicillin, ignoring the down-stream impact? What if, instead of looking at the issues with penicillin, they just kept selling *more* of it?

It's not dramatic to say that ignoring the reality of penicillin's vulnerabilities would have cost millions of lives. Instead, doctors faced reality, and worked on solving the problem.

Strangely enough, for a group of data-driven tech entrepreneurs, we're incredibly good at ignoring similar signs in our own businesses. We've created a software that we believe is somehow the world's next wonder drug, and we just keep selling it to the public. We'll ignore massive issues—in this case, churn—and just try to sell more of our wonder drug. All the while, our customers will grow resistant to our incredible platform, and we'll just keep selling more and more, hoping the downstream problems will go away.

Here's the reality. If customers are constantly leaving, particularly before they fully activate, more sales aren't going to fix anything. In fact, selling more will cause you to churn through the market faster, in much the same way that over-prescribing penicillin won't help cure certain illnesses.

> **More sales will not solve your activation problem...more sales will make it worse.**

It's time to stop the madness. It's time to stop using the short-term dopamine hit of a new sale as a replacement for doing the work that's required to build durable recurring revenue.

The Answer Is in the Math

Our company-building formula hinges on the Growth Ceiling calculation—it's the entire reason that the first two chapters of this book were dedicated to teaching you how to use it and describing the three levers that you can pull in order to grow your revenue and your customer base.

The reason this works is because unlike most "growth strategies," it's not based on someone's opinion—it's just the numbers. And so, when we see founders leaning into the "quick hit" of getting new sales as a solution to drowning out a churn problem, it hurts—because it's a glaring case of bad prioritization that will hurt the company in the long run.

> ## Don't build a growth strategy based on feelings. Build one based on math.

A Tale of Two Companies

Remember the exercise we did in chapter 2 that showed you how much churn can impact your bottom line? Well, we're going to hit it again—it's literally the foundation of building a durable company.

Take two founders in the exact same position—they've each got 1,000 customers, and they're each adding about 100 new ones per month. In both companies, customers aren't particularly happy—they're not activating, they're not getting value, and they're voting with their wallets: both company's churn rates are hovering around 10 percent.

- Total Customers: 1,000
- Churn Rate: 10% (100 customers lost)
- New Sales: 100
- Net Growth: 0 units

These companies are at their Growth Ceiling. They're losing the same amount of customers that they're gaining and are throwing cash into the fire every month (via their marketing and sales spend) simply to go sideways. It's a bad place to be.

Stuck At The Growth Ceiling

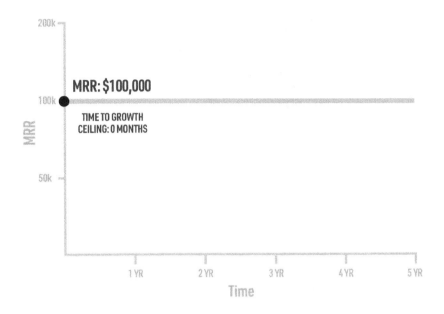

MRR: $100,000

TIME TO GROWTH
CEILING: 0 MONTHS

Now let's say that Founder A is going to keep their head in the sand—so they pull the lever that they've always pulled: **Getting More Customers.** Meanwhile, Founder B realizes that there's a ton of wasted opportunity happening after the sale, and that their product isn't working nearly well enough—so like Dan did in Flowtown, they choose to **Keep Customers Longer** by nailing their activation.

Let's say Founder A increases their new customers by 50 percent—which is a massive win. They're bringing in 150 new customers per month, but still sitting at 10 percent churn.

> In this scenario, by increasing sales by 50%, Founder A will push their Growth Ceiling out to about 22 months.

Growth Ceiling w/ More Sales

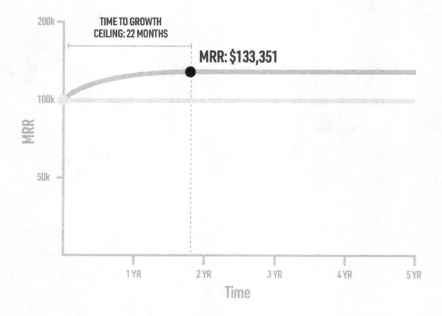

This looks good on the surface, but let's check out what Founder B is able to do:

Founder B, instead of increasing sales, keeps their new customers at the same 100 per month they've always had, but reduces churn from 10 percent to 5 percent monthly.

The result?

> **Founder B will push their Growth Ceiling out to about 55 months.**

Growth Ceiling w/ Improved Retention

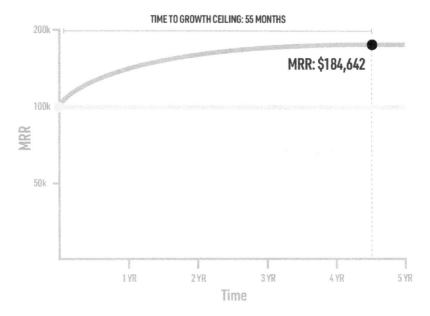

Here's the other issue: Founder A will have materially increased their sales and marketing spend, and they're still churning through 10 percent of their customers every single month.

> ## Trying to outpace a solvable churn problem with new sales means you're literally spending more money to let people down.

In a situation where you think you've gotten churn as low as you realistically can get it, ramping up sales and marketing is probably the right call (as long as you can afford it). But in a situation where you CAN reduce churn in a material way...you probably should.

In the example above, Founder B has added years to their growth curve—and they'll be stacking additional wins on top of it (like happy, engaged customers who are in it for the long haul). Most importantly, compared to Founder A's next plateau, Founder B's revenue will be about 40 percent higher before their next Growth Ceiling, meaning they'll have more cash on hand to invest in sales.

Alright—enough with the math (for now). We've explained to you (and proven to you, too) that there's a ton of opportunity after the sale...it's time to figure out why.

Why Don't Customers Activate?

Ever said any of these?

- "I have no idea why our users aren't smart enough to figure this out."
- "If they'd just read the docs, they'd know exactly how to use it."
- "There's no way these people can't figure out how to get set up—it's so obvious."

There's a reason for this: Johnny calls it the "Expert's Dilemma."

The Expert's Dilemma occurs when you've spent so much time solving a problem that you forget how to explain it to a beginner. And if you've ever tried to teach someone how to drive, you know exactly what we're talking about. You could probably drive to a dozen different places today without even consciously considering where you're going. By now, you probably have something like a built-in autopilot.

But when you're teaching someone to drive for the first time, it's a totally different game—suddenly, you have to remember to explain things like checking your mirrors regularly and how to deal with a flashing red light, even though these details seem obvious to you.

Onboarding is the same.

You've looked at your software and thought about solving a specific problem for years, so it's easy to forget that it's your customer's "first time out on the road." And whether you realize it or not, you've signed up to be their guide.

With that in mind, let's walk through the top reasons that your customers won't successfully activate—because if you've got an onboarding problem, it's likely in one of these three key areas.

You Don't Have Clear Instructions

It's easy to forget how complex our software platforms actually are. For a new user, it's like a trail that they've never walked before—the path might feel clear to us, but until you've done it a few times, you need a map. Even better, they need a GPS with turn-by-turn directions.

But instead of taking this approach, we frequently sign up a new customer, email them a link to log in, and leave them on a blank dashboard. No clear directions. No map. No GPS. Nothing.

We call this a "Dashboard Dump," it's one of the worst mistakes you could make in onboarding: In a Dashboard Dump, you walk a customer through a meticulously crafted and measured sales process, send them an email with a link which drops them off on a blank dashboard with no sample data and no instructions, and then get mad at them when they can't figure it out and want to cancel their subscription.

Imagine how angry you'd be if you bought a house full of furniture from IKEA and realized that they didn't give you any of the instructions. Now imagine that you had to keep paying for that furniture, every month...regardless of if you figured out how to put it together properly or not.

Crazy.

No matter how simple you think your platform is, assume it's ten times more complicated, and that no one, ever, will read any docs you send.

Steve Krug wrote an entire book on this called *Don't Make Me Think*. The entire focus of the book is on improving usability between humans and computers—specifically in the context of web-based software applications. He says it like this:

"The fact that the people who built the site didn't care enough to make things obvious—and easy—can erode our confidence in the [software] and the organization behind it."

It's not your users' job to "figure it out"—it's your job to give them the GPS and make sure they don't get lost.

You Made It Too Much Work

Oftentimes, we ask way too much of a brand-new user. Instead of putting them in the express lane to achieving First Value, you turn around and ask them to do more work. They've got to build an account, install a JavaScript snippet on their website, connect to Salesforce and map a bunch of fields, grant some permissions, invite their team, upload a profile picture...it's way too much, way too soon.

> **Your activation flow should be the minimum effective dose of configuration required to get the user to First Value.**

The first time your new customer logs in, they need a few, super simple next steps—and they should only be the steps that are specifically required to get them to First Value (and hooked on your product). Thinking back to the Red Napkin strategy, Taffer's strategy was to lead his customers down the path that would make them lifelong regulars. He knew that his immediate goal was three visits, so he made all three of those visits as easy and enjoyable as possible.

In his *New York Times* bestseller, *Atomic Habits*, James Clear talks about the four laws of behavior change, then puts them into two contexts—depending on whether you want to create a habit or break a habit:

Create a new habit:

1. Make it obvious.
2. Make it attractive.
3. Make it easy.
4. Make it satisfying.

Conversely, if you want to break a habit, Clear says to simply do the opposite of those things.

Break a habit:

1. Make it invisible.
2. Make it unattractive.
3. Make it difficult.
4. Make it unsatisfying.

This is an incredible litmus test for your onboarding. Which list do you think your activation flow most closely resembles? If the steps that are required for your customer to reach First Value are invisible, unattractive, difficult to accomplish, and without a big payoff at the end...it shouldn't be a mystery why they're canceling after a few months.

But if you make this initial flow easy...or better yet, fun...they'll sail through the first steps and get hooked on the value...for good.

You Didn't Install Any Guardrails

When we talked about your marketing funnel in chapter 4, we ran through a number of strategies to keep people locked in and moving to the next stage in the buyer's journey—lead magnets to get their information, retargeting ads, email sequences, case studies...each one of them is a tool to be applied at a specific stage of the funnel to achieve a specific goal.

Those tools act as guardrails—to make sure that the potential buyer doesn't drop out of the funnel and disappear. Turns out, the same strategy works here too—you need to install some guardrails to keep your brand-new user moving towards their First Value moment.

The right guardrails to keep someone on the path to First Value are usually made up of four tools:

1.   **A well-designed onboarding flow** that points them towards the First Value moment
2.   **In-app prompts** to make sure they know what to do next
3.   **Trigger-based emails** to pull them back into the platform if they get stuck
4.   **Customer support that's readily available** if they can't figure out how to move forward

Tools like these help keep your customers in the "activation funnel"—and when implemented properly, will directly impact your churn numbers.

Canva, for example, has some really interesting elements in their onboarding flow that are designed to help save their new user's time. As an example, they grab your email domain that you signed up with, and if it matches a company website, they'll scrape the company name and logo to show you a pre-populated brand kit as part of the signup flow.[9]

---

[9] https://www.useronboard.com/how-canva-onboards-new-users/?slide=63

Canva's Easy Onboarding

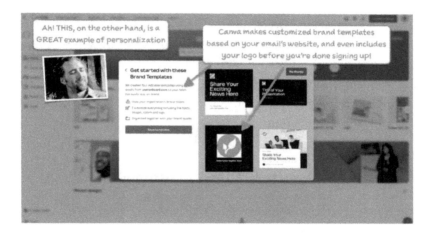

They also pre-populate some of their templates—for instance, if you choose a doc, it'll load a placeholder quote in the header so you're not staring at a blank page (sounds familiar if you remember our Flowtown story).

> **Populating sample data is a great way to avoid the Dashboard Dump.**

This is all done by design—and Melanie Perkins, Canva's incredible co-founder and CEO, described exactly why they do it this way in a podcast with Reid Hoffman (LinkedIn's co-founder and host of the *Masters of Scale* podcast):

> People had been told their entire lives that they weren't creative, that they didn't have a design bone in their body. And all of a sudden, they were put with this tool, and they were scared to actually use it. And so, we had to spend a lot of time refining that user experience when people first jumped into the product, to ensure that when people came in, within a couple of minutes, they

were having fun, they felt playful, they felt that they could actually do this.

But the best guardrails aren't just inside the software—they will guide the user when they're on platform and will pull them back in when they stray. Our good friend Brad Redding, who is both a former client and SaaS Academy coach, has really nailed this—and if you think that your software is "too technical" for these principles to work for you...Brad will show you how you're wrong.

"We Busted Our Asses to Get Them to Activate."

Brad Redding is the co-founder and CEO of Elevar—a software platform that helps eCommerce brands accurately track their conversions—and he had a serious activation problem.

The problem was terrifying: when they started measuring their First Value moment, they realized that one out of every two customers was totally failing to activate.

Imagine the weight of this realization for a second. Since we know that customers who fail to activate rarely make it longer than 90 days, Brad found himself in a situation where he was driving demand in the market, moving ideal customers down the funnel, converting them into paying customers...and realizing that HALF of them were going to churn out in the blink of an eye.

> The first thing to understand is that Elevar is a very technical product. We're sending data from point A to point B, which means that we need to get things integrated, get conversion tracking set up...there's a lot to do there. And we work with a lot of platforms.

And at this point in time, the product wasn't focusing on a single use case—because they didn't know which platform was important to the user.

Brad and his team did the next right thing—they talked to all the customers who had failed to activate to figure out what the issue was. And the biggest thing they heard was that there were too many options and that they weren't sure what to do next.

> ## If a user can log in for the first time and "do anything they want" . . . you're missing the opportunity to truly guide them.

He fixed this in two ways. The first was to move the customer support up in the onboarding flow. They started doing 1:1 onboarding for their customers, and eventually started charging for it (which we'll cover in depth in chapter 11).

But they also started collecting better data on the way in.

When a new customer activated, they had them indicate which platform was most important for them to integrate. And then they built the onboarding so that it focused only on that one platform until it was "plugged in." The customer started to get conversation data out of Elevar—which is the whole point of the software in the first place.

But it wasn't just about the onboarding flow—with technical products, users are a lot more likely to leave after their first login (they might need to get someone else on their team or go read some help articles...it's more complex than scheduling a Tweet).

For Brad and his team, the answer was in-app prompts and email campaigns based off of the completion of specific onboarding steps.

> We now keep our email activation flows very specific, triggering the customer to go from point A to point B, with emails and in-app prompts, or other triggers. And we're hitting them with very specific cues. And we just try to bust our asses as hard as we can to

just get that customer onboarded and fully activated as quickly as possible.

A few months after making these changes, Brad and his team had increased successful new user activation to nearly 80 percent.

Notice the sequencing here. They started by talking to churned customers to figure out what went wrong—and they worked backwards from those data points until they'd fixed the problem in the software.

We couldn't have come up with a better execution if we tried.

Do you remember the Builder's Curse from chapter 5? Where you fall in love with your product because it was so hard to build and end up feature-dumping during a sales call? Yeah, it exists here too.

> **We get so wrapped up in the beauty of our platform that we forget what really matters: fixing the customer's pain.**

And the way Brad did it is the right way—by looking at the data. Customers don't want to be forced to try every single feature of your platform in order to figure out which one solves their problem. They'll get there eventually, but just like a restaurant, your job is to give them a great first meal. If the experience is enjoyable, they'll keep coming back for more—but you just can't cram the whole menu into one dinner.

Alright—we've talked a lot about *why* this is important—and now it's time for the how.

There are really two main jobs to be done here—figuring out what your First Value moment is and doing the work to steer all of your new users to that moment as quickly and reliably as possible.

And we're about to give you the framework that'll help you nail them both.

It's A Hurdle Race to First Value

The concept here is easy: find the one action that every one of your successful customers takes. The one achievement that gets them excited. The one experience that shows them a clear ROI on the platform they just purchased, and that makes them want to continue using it forever.

From there, build a path for every customer to achieve the same breakthrough. Otherwise, you've got to assume that they'll exit your world, and drift off into the abyss.

Make that path super simple, clearly laying out each step. Once they reach one checkpoint, make it obvious where the next one is. It's much easier to keep going when you can see where you need to go next.

A key principle here is the Rule of Three:

> **For most SaaS products, there can only be 3 steps between a customer and their First Value moment.**

Ideally, each step is pretty easy to complete—shored up with guides and guardrails—and the journey to the First Value moment remains straightforward and uncomplicated.

The Activation Builder

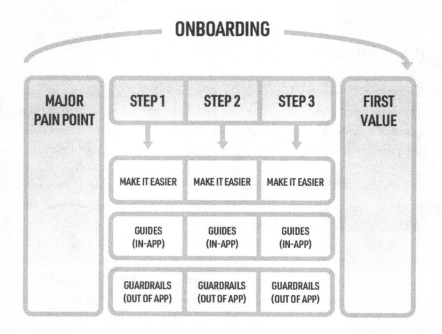

To be clear, the constraint is that the **First Value moment should be the same for every single customer**—just like it is for every guest at a restaurant. In the restaurant example, the First Value was when the customer completes their third meal. For Twitter, every new user needed to follow a few of their favorite accounts so the algorithm could serve them content that keeps them on-platform. For Flowtown, Dan needed each new user to schedule a Tweet straight away if they were going to remain customers.

And if you think that your software is too complex for this, consider Brad—who integrates with over fifty other software platforms...his First Value moment was to get the first integration completed—which meant that choosing which integration to set up was simply one of the checkpoints.

Every customer who buys from you has something that they need to achieve. In his book *Hooked: How to Build Habit-Forming Products*, Nir Eyal says it like this: "What is the simplest action that users can take in anticipation of a reward, and how can you simplify your product to make this action easier?"

What follows on the next few pages is the exact framework that Brad used to juice his activation rate to almost 80 percent at Elevar.

Step 1: Find the First Value moment

As you probably guessed, this is the critical first step—we've got to figure out the "one thing"—the one moment that every new user needs to experience in order to see the value in your SaaS platform. Sometimes it's obvious—but oftentimes, it's not (or we have limiting beliefs about how "every user is different").

> **The thing your users want might be different than what you *think* they want. And to figure it out...you need to ask them.**

Brad asked his churned customers what they were trying to achieve and how they got let down in the process—and he was able to zero in on getting that first integration set up as his value moment. Twitter thought that Tweeting was the First Value moment (which feels logical) until they realized that users valued consumption over creation.

> **Your users made a purchase to solve a problem—and you need to figure out how they expect it to work.**

By figuring out the one thing that your top users do to get value from your platform, you can build an activation flow that funnels all new users towards that same outcome. And if you're not sure what to ask them, you can snag our customer interview swipe file at softwarebook.com/activation - but here are a few questions to get you started:

1. How would you describe our product in your own words?
2. What's the problem that <product> solves for you?
3. What was the exact moment when you realized that <product> would solve the problem?
4. What were the steps that you had to take to get <outcome>?
5. If <product> could only do one thing for you, what would be most important?

If you're thinking about simply loading these five questions into a survey and blasting it out to your customers...you're not yet giving user activation the attention that it deserves. Every company has a set of best customers. The ones you would clone. Who talk about you on social media. Who give you glowing reviews, tell people how amazing you are, and don't consume 83 percent of your support bandwidth.

If you don't know who these customers are, that's step one. Make the list. And then reach out to them personally. Live conversations can shift in ways that you can't anticipate—and it'll teach you things that you'd never have thought to ask in a transactional email survey. Truly listen to them and figure out the "one thing" that they want.

Audit Your Click Stream

If you've got a SaaS platform with users, you need to have analytics software installed. It's one line of JavaScript and a little bit of cash in exchange for all the intel you ever wanted. Ideally, you'll choose a solution that tracks the click stream (what people clicked on, and in what order). It should also capture session recordings (screen recordings of users navigating your platform).

We can almost guarantee that your customers aren't using your solution the way you thought they would. Watching session recordings is one of the most illuminating things you can do to understand your software through the eyes of your customers.

Step 2: Nail the Three Stepping Stones

Once you've figured out the "one thing" that your customers want, you need to build the stepping stones to get them there.

We talked about the Rule of Three—that there should only be three steps between your customer and their First Value moment—but that doesn't mean that there has to be three.

It can be two steps. Or even one.

Establishing these stepping stones can require additional work in your product, your onboarding process, and your customer success process too. But it all starts with figuring out how things should work and building backwards from there.

A quick piece of advice here: don't get paralyzed by chasing perfection. There's a good chance that you're miles away from what you consider the perfect three-step onboarding flow. That's okay—it's a journey. But you need to know what you're building towards so you can keep making progress...which is what we'll cover next.

Step 3: Guide the Steps to Make Them Easy

The goal here is to make each stepping stone incredibly easy for your users.

This is where the real product work comes in—bulldozing roadblock after roadblock until your user activation isn't just possible...it's inevitable.

By watching session recordings, reviewing click streams, and talking to both happy customers as well as customers who fail to activate, you'll be able to identify the friction points in each of your stepping stones.

And once you've identified them, you need to annihilate them.

Here are a few ways to do it:

Install Some Signposts

If you've ever hiked along an unmarked trail, you know the underlying anxiety that comes along with wondering if you're lost or not. Sure, maybe you're a land-nav expert who can survive for weeks in the woods with some chewing gum and a wet match, but your users probably aren't.

They need some signposts—some clear guidance, inside of your software platform, to point them directly to the next action they need to take. They need clear, direct signals: "Do this. Now, do that." The best products in the world have a step-by-step onboarding wizard that shows them exactly how to complete each of their stepping stone actions—and you should build towards having the same thing.

> **Tooltips and help text can be a band-aid, but they won't fix a bad onboarding flow.**

Don't just install some pop ups and consider it "fixed"—because we've seen that enough times to know that it won't work all by itself...it's just an ingredient. There's a difference between serving a great meal and just handing someone a rib. Your product should guide them through the flow from start to finish—and the experience should be awesome.

Replace the Inputs

Your goal should be to eliminate as many inputs as possible, and replace them with one of three things:

1. Automations
2. Integrations
3. Facilitated Experiences (via your success team)

Canva, who we mentioned earlier, is a great example of this. They know that someone who signs up for a team plan probably has a company, and the user wants to keep their designs on brand.

And if we had to guess, they probably started with an input-based flow. Upload your logo. Enter your company name. Pick your colors. Upload your fonts. And so on and so forth.

By replacing those inputs with automations and integrations, they now pull the company name from the onboarding form, the logo and colors from your company website, and surface a mostly-completed brand kit that the user can edit and save (vs. creating from scratch)—getting the user quickly and seamlessly through that activation step.

Compare that to the experience of a user that's now searching Dropbox for the version of their logo with the transparent background...who then gets a Slack message, gets distracted, and falls out of the onboarding flow...and you'll see why this is so important to focus on.

Simple automations like this show your customer that you know what you're doing, and that you want them to focus on your product. They help cut friction to zero—which is a critical outcome if you're looking to maximize your Activation Rate.

Step 4: Install Guardrails to Keep Users Engaged

This was one of the key steps that helped Brad—and it's incredibly important, especially if you have a technically complex product.

> ## The more complicated your onboarding is, the more likely they have to leave your platform to do it.

Which means that you need some mechanisms to make sure you can pull them back into the process and keep things on track.

Here are a few ways you can do it:

Event-Driven Emails

Think about big e-commerce operations like Target and Amazon...they shoot you an email if you abandon your shopping cart, if you look at a product that you don't purchase, or even if you quietly think about a product within five feet of an Alexa device (creepy).

There's a lot to learn there—and in SaaS onboarding, it shows up as event-driven email sequences.

Instead of just sending your users emails based on time (i.e., X days after signup), figure out how far along the activation flow they should be—and then change the email based on whether or not they're on track or off track.

If they should have knocked out two of their stepping stones by day 7, and they haven't done it yet, you should be sending them a customized email to help get them unblocked (and ideally having a CS person reach out as well).

> **Your new users *will* fall off the path—it's your job to have a plan to get them back on track.**

Get Their Digits

We're big believers in getting people's phone numbers—especially for your customers. If they're purchasing software from you, they're hiring your tool to get them a result. Why would you take options off the table if they need help?

Properly configured text outreach campaigns have roughly triple the deliverability of their email counterparts—so if you're having trouble keeping your customers focused on activation, you're missing a huge opportunity by not doing this.

It also lets you overdeliver by offering phone support—which is pretty tough to do if you only know how to reach your customers via email.

The Most Common Pitfall in SaaS

Under-investing in user onboarding is one of the most common mistakes we see founders make. We focus so much on marketing and sales, and if churn is too high, we wonder if our prices are too high, if we need faster support replies, or a thousand other things before we dig into the product itself.

By taking the stepping stone approach to user activation, you can make sure that the vast majority of your users get to their First Value moment as quickly and reliably as possible—which is one of the most high-leverage improvements you can make to reduce churn, retain customers longer, and build an incredible reputation for your business.

Pro Tip: When Brad started working on this, his first move was to offer 1:1 implementation while he figured out how to improve the product.

Turns out, the implementation was so effective that he kept it—and now charges for it—as part of his onboarding workflow. For a few hundred bucks, Brad's team provides the white-glove service that many of his customers want. They're basically paying to be activated more quickly.

We're going to go super deep on this topic in chapter 11—it's an incredibly effective follow-on to what we covered here. But your RETENTION problem isn't solved yet.

Activation is just the first step to building durable recurring revenue. It's something that has to be world-class, but it's also short lived. In order to truly **Keep Customers Longer**, you've got to play the long game...and in the next chapter, you'll meet a founder who added $500,000 in ARR by taking a proactive approach to his customer success—and you'll also learn exactly how he did it.

5 Hot Principles

1. **Know your First Value moment:** Get to know the habits and experiences of your best customers and distill it down to the exact moment when they'll consistently say, "Oh, I get it now!"—and focus *everything* in your onboarding flow towards getting your new users to experience that moment as fast as possible.

2. **Install instrumentation:** You're running a technology business—use it to your advantage. Get some software in place to track click streams and store session recordings so you can stop guessing how people use your software and actually learn it based on facts—which will help you build an activation process that's tighter than it's ever been before.

3. **Nail the stepping stones:** Identify the three steps (max) that every new user needs to take in order to get to the First Value moment. You should know the order that they need to happen in, how long each one should take, and the biggest friction points

that stand in the way—which should be high on your product roadmap to improve.

4. **Keep them on track:** Install the guardrails that are required to keep users on the path—dedicated onboarding flows, help text, event-driven emails, proactive text outreach...whatever it takes to pull them in and get them to the activation finish line.

5. **Measure activation weekly:** Like Brad did, you should be measuring activation every week as a company. How many new users *should* have completed activation last week vs. how many *did*? Don't over-engineer it—but if you want to improve it, the first thing you need to do is pay attention to it.

The Next Right Move

There are a few action items here, depending on where you are in your activation journey—they need to be done in order.

Head to softwarebook.com/activation to download the Activation Builder™, which will walk you through everything you need to put this chapter into play. We've also got a few great examples and resources to help you see what world-class onboarding looks like.

Step 1: If you don't know what your First Value moment is, figure that out before you do anything else.

Talk to customers, audit usage via click streams and session recordings, and figure out what the most common "ah-ha" moment is. Don't overthink it...you can always change it if you end up wrong but do your best to get it right.

My First Value moment is: _____

Step 2: Design the three "stepping stones" to take a new user from first login to "hell yeah."

When you know what they are, write them down—this is the critical journey that you need to build.

Stepping Stone #1: _____

Stepping Stone #2: _____

Stepping Stone #3: _____

Step 3: Select _one improvement_ that you can implement quickly.

It's easy to get crushed by the weight of "I need to rebuild everything"—that's not useful if you can't take immediate action. Figure out the _next right move_ to eliminate your _one_ biggest friction point and ship it as quickly as possible.

The next action I'll take to improve my activation is: _____

CHAPTER 7

Finding Your C.H.I.

"If your churn isn't in the single digits, it's absolutely the only thing you should be fixing right now."[x]
JOSH PIGFORD, founder and CEO of Maybe and founder of Baremetrics

ANDRE CVIJOVIC IS THE FOUNDER and CEO of Referrizer, which helps brick-and-mortar businesses grow their revenue with a platform that manages their reviews and drives killer marketing campaigns. It sounds awesome (and it is)—but when we first met him, he was struggling with churn...to the point where he was turning over his *entire* customer base on an annual basis.

He'd had enough. After running the numbers over and over again (and a bunch of late night google searches about how to stop churn), he decided it was time to get serious. All of the "hacks" and "quick fixes" felt half-baked, because they were missing a key piece of the puzzle:

> **To truly get a handle on retention, your customer success efforts need to be *proactive*.**

It's easy to say, but tough to implement. Which is why most people who are publishing content that ranks for "how to stop churn" don't write about it. In his words, he got tons of ideas, but "no solutions."

What we're about to teach you in this chapter is the solution you've been wishing for.

It's not sexy. It doesn't use some cutting-edge AI technology or fancy marketing strategy. But like most things in life, the fundamentals of a great strategy are timeless. And Andre is proof of this—within a month of implementing exactly what we're about to show you in this chapter, he'd reduced his churn to the point where he was retaining twenty more customers per month.

At an average lifetime value of $2,000, those customers he retained were creating an extra $40,000 in MRR for Referrizer. Almost half a million dollars in additional revenue—from customers he'd already won.

We're just going to keep saying it—*success starts after the sale is made.*

***

"Be proactive" is the first habit that famed author Stephen Covey offers in his classic book, *The 7 Habits of Highly Effective People*. It's a straightforward instruction and can be applied in almost any situation.

To think through what it means to be proactive with your retention strategy, we can boil it down to a couple of key questions:

What if you could determine who was at risk of leaving before they even thought about it?

What if you could proactively reach out to the customers who need more attention to keep them fully engaged?

It's not only possible...it's something that we think should be required for every SaaS company on Earth (that cares about their customers). And if you want to see what "world class" looks like here, look no further than HubSpot.

Finding Your C.H.I.

Dharmesh Shah (co-founder and CTO of HubSpot) is well known for many things—but one of them is how he pioneered HubSpot's Customer Health Index, or C.H.I.

"If I could just point back to one thing that made HubSpot tick...this would be way, way up on the list."[xi]

And since HubSpot is now helping over 200,000 happy customers (and has a market cap of over $30 billion) . . . it's probably a good idea to listen up on this one. Here's the big idea:

> **You can create one metric to figure out exactly how happy your customers are.**

The way that Shah explains it is that it's a single number that's designed to show how likely a customer is to stick around another month despite having the opportunity to cancel. It's created from a mix of data, including *frequency* (i.e., how often they are using the software) and *features* (i.e., are they receiving value from using the platform).

HubSpot boils all this down to one number, ranging from 0 to 100. Every customer gets a score based on their underlying data, and they rally their entire team to improve it—because they know that customers below a certain threshold are more likely to churn. Happy customers, on the other hand, drive increased retention, which in turn builds durable revenue.

What if you had that level of insight for your own business? What would it change for you?

Here's the craziest thing: customers aren't even aware that their C.H.I. is declining. HubSpot is essentially reading their customers' minds by watching how they're interacting with the software. They can be truly proactive—solving problems before the customer even knows they exist.

Building a SaaS company that consistently retains and expands customer accounts means developing a C.H.I.-style metric. One number that's so insightful that you know a customer is frustrated even before they do. When you do this right, you'll be able to consistently and accurately monitor how your customers feel...and you can do it *at scale*.

In the last chapter, we talked about how important it is to get your customers to their First Value moment as quickly as possible. If you don't do it, they're almost always gone within 90 days—that's the reality. But in order to truly build lifelong fans, you've got to keep the value coming— week over week, month over month, year over year...and this chapter is all about making sure you know if you're getting the job done or not.

> **Monthly recurring revenue is only useful if it *keeps recurring*.**

The key interactions that go into your C.H.I. will vary from company to company—we'll walk you through that in a bit. But before we get to the nuts and bolts, let's walk through how to think about segmenting your customers (and the actions that should be taken as a result).

The Customer Engagement Elevator™

Look, if all this sounds like you need a data scientist and a team of software engineers to build it...don't worry. As usual, we'll give you the minimum effective dose of what you need to start segmenting your customers and getting ahead of churn.

Here's how to think about it:

The Customer Engagement Elevator

CUSTOMER ENGAGEMENT ELEVATOR

ADVOCATES | PURPLE

ALL-STARS | GREEN

AT RISK | YELLOW

UNENGAGED | RED

Imagine your customers are on four different levels of an office building. The top floor, overlooking the city with the best view, is where your Advocates are. These are your happiest, most engaged customers. They're all the way up—loving your product, leaving you great reviews, logging in every day and using key features, and supporting you and your company in every way possible. We call these "purple customers"—they sit outside of the traditional traffic light system, because they're that important (and we'll teach you why they're so important in the next chapter—it's wild).

Right below them are your All Stars. They're using the product the same way that the Advocates are—but they're not as vocal about their success (yet). They're still fully activated, happy customers, and their usage metrics are dialed in and showing the value they're getting. These are your "Green Customers."

On the next floor down is your set of Average customers—the ones who we consider to be "Yellow" on the traffic light system. They're not at the bottom, but they're not fully engaged either. They might be logging in less often than they used to, or only using one feature and ignoring the rest of the platform. There's an opportunity to move them up—but left unattended, they'll usually end up at the bottom.

And then there's the bottom floor. The unengaged customers that are definitely a churn risk. They will need a lot of love in order to get them moving up again, and some of them may even be a lost cause. It's a tough place to be—especially if you have a lot of your customers hanging out down there. Naturally, these are our "Red Customers."

> ## Churn comes from customers that are on the bottom 2 floors.

Without changing anything, your At-Risk customers are basically guaranteed to churn—it's probably a miracle they're still paying you to begin with. And the Average customers that could be salvaged—and maybe turned into All Stars or even Advocates—well, a bunch of them are likely to bounce too.

To bring people up to the next level, you've got to do three things:

1. **Research:** Understand what behaviors represent healthy customers
2. **Lift:** Lead your customers to take more of those actions
3. **Monitor:** Regularly track your customer base to ensure that the actions are maintained

In HubSpot's case, their C.H.I. has many inputs—it's a calculated average of a number of customer actions—based on both frequency and on features. And the output of that calculation tells them, with alarming accuracy, how likely customers were to churn.

The good news is although their metric consists of a bunch of different touch points that are all calculated into a single number, yours doesn't have to be nearly as complicated. But you do need something directionally similar—a metric that tells you how happy your customers are. By proactively monitoring the C.H.I. of your customers, you can see potential churn coming—often before the customer even knows they're in the danger zone.

You're not going to nail your Customer Happiness Index the first time out.

You're going to get it wrong. It's practically a guarantee. And it's fine— because even Shah says that HubSpot adjusts their C.H.I. every four to six months—refining it is part of the process. So even if you're just measuring logins, the key is to just start—so that you can build the muscle of trying to figure out how to re-engage your customers before their excitement fizzles out forever.

Here's a closer look at the model, using HubSpot as an example:

- **Research:** HubSpot found the key actions that equate to a happy customer and boiled it down to a single numerical score between 0 and 100 (C.H.I.). They refine it over time, returning to this Research step a few times per year.

- **Lift:** The team at HubSpot proactively engages customers in ways that make them "happy"—meaning they work to elevate the C.H.I. (because they know the actions that drive it).

- **Monitor:** Everyone at HubSpot knows the C.H.I. of the customer base—and because it's tied to customer satisfaction, they can all rally behind why it's important—and do whatever it takes to increase it.

Research: Use SWAG

In HubSpot's case, they're using a calculation based off of a bunch of metrics that have evolved over time. It's not just one interaction. But if you're starting with nothing, you can just pick one metric that you think will correlate to a happy customer.

As the founder, you probably have an idea of what this key metric might be. Think about "what success means" for your product. If you're a social network like LinkedIn, it might be daily active users or posts on the platform. If you're a lead generation platform for local businesses, it might be the number of leads generated over the past fourteen days per account. You get the idea.

You can get super analytical with this. You could look at your best users, audit all the click streams and how frequently they're using certain features, calculate a weighted average...and yes, you'll probably get there at some point.

But if this type of tracking is new to you, and you don't already have a clear dashboard to break your customers into levels based on some sort of data...we recommend you pick your one metric via the SWAG method:

> **A SWAG is a Scientific Wild-Ass Guess, and it's usually more accurate than you think.**

For example, one of our early-stage clients (we'll call her Miranda) wasn't sure exactly which features would be a good example of recurring value from her platform. Most of what she could measure was based on generating data for a real estate deal that probably only happened once every sixty days or so, and she was feeling stuck on how to create a useful C.H.I.

But despite the fact that her "value delivery" was pretty infrequent, the users had to log into the platform—in many cases, on a daily basis—in order to take the actions that *led up* to the value moment.

In the absence of a perfectly tuned weighted average formula, she took a SWAG, and decided that her happiest customers were logging into the platform on a daily basis. The less-than-happy customer was probably in there once a week. And the customers who weren't engaged were rarely logging in.

In Miranda's case, measuring login frequency was the next right move for setting up her C.H.I.:

- All Stars and Advocates: At least 1 login in the past 24 hours
- At-Risk: At least 1 login in the past 7 days
- Unengaged: 0 logins in the past 7 days

Yes, it can be that simple. In the same way that you thought about your First Value moment, you've got to remember that this is an imperfect science. You'll get it wrong the first time, but the goal here is to *take action*—and improve over time.

The Pizza Meter

In the 1990s, Frank Meeks owned dozens of Domino's Pizza stores in the D.C. area. He came up with a simple metric to determine the state of affairs for the entire human race...and it was called the Pizza Meter.

Being in D.C., the staff at the Capitol, the White House, and the Pentagon would order from Meeks' stores whenever they had to pull an all-nighter. Meeks quickly discovered that whenever there was a national crisis announced, pizza sales from specific stores had spiked—the night before. Critical personnel would shut themselves in and work all night. And what's the best food in the world when you're awake in the wee hours of the night handling a global crisis?

Domino's pizza.

On an average night, Meeks said the White House would order about fifty pizzas. The night before the Clinton-Lewinsky scandal broke? They ordered over *900*. In the three days leading up to Clinton's impeachment,

Capitol Hill ordered almost ten times their usual amount. And on March 23, 1999, the night before the U.S. bombed Yugoslavia, the Pentagon set its record—800 pizzas.

Turns out, whenever the world was in crisis, the Pizza Meter knew it before we did.

Less Is More

The point is this: your key metric doesn't have to be fancy in order to be accurate.

Logins can work really well—especially if you're comparing it against not measuring anything at all. One company we talked to uses "time spent to complete a task" as a key metric. They measured how long it takes users to complete a certain task, compared the customers they were retaining vs. the ones they were losing, and realized that the canceled customers took much longer to complete the same task.

What do you think they did next? Set up trigger emails to help the customers along once their "time to complete" hit a certain threshold—and used that average threshold to calculate their C.H.I.

> ## Don't spend a ton of time developing something complicated. Keep it simple. Do less. And do it fast.

"But what do I do when I'm ready to graduate from a SWAG?"

It's the same strategy that we talked about in the last chapter: *ask the people who pay you.*

Look at how your top customers use the platform. Figure out which features your best people use, how often they use them, and how often they log in.

Then, look at your *worst* customers. The ones you know in your heart are about to churn (even if you can't prove it yet). Look at their stats for the same data points...because there will be a big difference between the two if you've picked the right metric.

And if not? Keep digging—because **success leaves clues**. It's your job to find them.

A world-class C.H.I. in a more mature operation consists of both *activity* data (how often people are logging in and using the software) and feature usage data (how often they're achieving key outcomes from the software itself). You'll also see companies adding additional dimensions, such as the last NPS score, and even subjective ratings from account managers based on 1:1 interactions.

Regardless of how complicated (or not complicated) your C.H.I. calculation is, the goal remains the same—to move as many users as possible up to the next level. So, by focusing on what your all-star users are already doing, you'll be pointed in the right direction from the get-go.

Lift: Use Customer Problems to Dazzle

Adii Pienaar is one of those founders who just oozes inspiration from every pore. He's a serial SaaS founder (WooCommerce, Conversio, and Cogsy)—and has also successfully exited all three. He's also the author of *Life Profitability: The New Measure of Entrepreneurial Success*, a former client and coach, and a great friend. He's the total package.

In his first company, Adii discovered a simple truth that he's been carrying with him through every business he's ever built. It's a crazy simple paradigm, but one that he says has been critical to his success:

When a customer has a problem, it's the perfect opportunity to dazzle them.

If there's an issue, or something's broken, or the customer just can't figure out how to do the thing they're trying to do—it's the exact moment where you can swoop in to create a memorable experience. Whether they'll admit it or not, your customers understand that hiccups happen. They end up with trouble logging in, or an email that was unclear, or an integration that bugs out. And when these things happen, Adii seizes the moment and uses them to build positive, lasting memories.

Disney does this all the time at their theme parks. If a kid is crying, or someone's airline loses their luggage, or someone drops an ice cream cone...just wait thirty seconds. A Disney "cast member" will swoop in and solve the problem by offering something that's likely inexpensive—but perfectly timed. Maybe it's a free cookie, an extra Lightning Lane pass, a fresh ice cream cone, or even a whole new outfit.

The smallest gesture can mean the world in the middle of a dilemma.

The true magic is that the thing that was a bad experience is now the highlight of someone's $5,000 vacation. All for a few bucks and a little bit of effort. Disney is capitalizing on turning negative moments into cherished memories.

And it's NOT actually magic—you can do the same thing in your business...as long as you're looking for it.

Finding the Opportunities

There's been a theme through this whole chapter: *be proactive*. And when it comes to looking for opportunities to "dazzle" your customers, it really matters.

Sure, there's a *reactive* component to it—you want to make it right when your software has a bug, or something doesn't work right—the tech version of dropping your ice cream cone. But the next level is based on *proactivity*—which means finding the customers who aren't using as much of the software as they could be and helping them improve their workflows and get more value from what they're already paying for.

Even if your C.H.I. is super basic and only tracking the frequency of logins, you can still do this simply by reaching out to customers who are starting to drop off and offering to help them. And as it evolves to track feature usage, you can get even more targeted—offering specific types of help to get the customer hooked on more of your core features over time—which will increase the likelihood that they'll stick around...and move them up from "At-Risk" to "All Star."

This is the big goal here—the more you can see what your customers are using (and aren't using), the more targeted and proactive your assistance can be. This will, in turn, let you create more magical moments for them, keep them at "all-star" status, and transform them from lukewarm users into raving fans.

Monitor: Traffic Lights = Daily Actions

All this talk about "finding problems" is great, but it won't mean anything if we don't build a simple system to operationalize it. Johnny built this masterfully in his first company Silvertrac—he had the usage data feeding into a single C.H.I., which then was surfaced on a dashboard for his customer success team to use...every single day.

> **Your entire customer base should be classified as purple, green, yellow, or red. And your job is to move yellows up to greens, and reds up to yellows[10].**

It might feel tempting to focus mostly on the reds—and yes, they should get some effort—but you likely have a ton of opportunity in the yellows. As you tweak this measurement over time, you'll find that your yellow group are the ones who aren't thrilled but aren't angry. They might use one feature and log in periodically, but they're not using all of your features or logging in daily.

There's a lot of untapped growth sitting in the gap between yellow and green.

Data Isn't Enough by Itself

When you first start reaching out to truly unengaged customers, you might get some negative responses. If you make phone calls to a few dozen "red" accounts, you're almost guaranteed to have a couple that say something like, "Glad you called—I've been meaning to cancel. Can you handle that for me?" Sigh.

It's not what you wanted. It'll feel like a bummer. But there's some good news:

> **You are creating the chance to learn firsthand why customers are leaving.**

Remember Josh from Baremetrics—the founder we quoted at the beginning of this chapter? Early on in his journey, he was dealing with a

---

[10] What about turning greens into purples, you ask? That's what the entire *next* chapter is about.

tough churn problem—in his words, "It had been creeping up from an already-less-than-stellar 6 percent to an unsustainable 13 percent." And they'd tried all the usual plays to figure out why—form fields, asking for feedback, reaching out to churned customers…the whole nine yards. But they still weren't learning enough to understand the problem.

So, they did something drastic. They removed the option to cancel online and required people to set up a call instead. For a monthly subscription software at his price point, this was pretty unconventional. But listen:

> The very first thing we did was remove the ability to cancel your account yourself. I know. Gasp! Heresy! Treason! But the reality was, our free form "let us know why you're canceling" text box wasn't cutting it. We just weren't getting anything remotely useful when it came to understanding exactly why people were canceling.

According to the blog that Josh wrote on the topic, his team didn't try to talk people out of canceling. They genuinely just wanted information on what they could do differently next time. And the insights they received were invaluable. For one, they found out that many people were leaving because they wanted one key feature—which was on the roadmap for the following month. Hearing this, 15 percent of those customers stayed—which never would have happened if Josh and his team hadn't gotten them on the phone.

Secondly, the whole team gained a ground-level understanding of the features that customers needed. When we combine a C.H.I. with 1:1 customer conversations, you'll build an incredible engine for capturing insights—which is exactly what Josh's team did here.

We're not saying that you, as the founder, need to handle every cancellation personally. But taking care of a handful of them might help you understand what's going on with your product and your customers— and you'll likely have a different lens on it compared to your team.

Oh, and P.S.—with the info that he learned from talking to these customers, Josh was able to reduce his churn from the 13 percent he mentioned all the way back down to 5 percent—in his own words, it saved his business (which he then went on to successfully sell a few years later).

Progress Over Perfection

There are two main issues when we coach founders to set this type of dashboard up:

1. They don't do it.
2. They overcomplicate it to the point where it's incredibly hard...and then they don't do it.

We know it can be tough to prioritize this kind of work against all your shiny new features...but trust us when we say that it's worth stepping back from your backlog for a couple days to set something like this up. And we want to make it as easy as possible for you—which is why we built a template specifically for building a C.H.I. metric (available for you at softwarebook.com/health).

> **A small improvement in churn has a huge impact on your Growth Ceiling—prioritize accordingly.**

And remember—you'll definitely, positively, absolutely get it wrong the first time out. You're not going to go from zero to "laser accurate predictor of all churn" on the first try. That's why we recommend starting with either measuring straight usage or taking a SWAG—and then adjusting over time.

Think about scientists and researchers—as they push the limits of knowledge in their fields, they start with a hypothesis. Then come the dozens (or hundreds) of experiments that it takes to prove or disprove their hypothesis (a.k.a. their SWAG). It's simple when you boil it down—scientists prove a theory by running experiments, over and over again.

And you are a scientist of SaaS. You should approach this work the same way—hypothesize, experiment, and iterate. It's not complicated to start, and the benefits are well worth your time and budget.

How do you know if it's working? Just look at the C.H.I. score of your customers who are canceling. If you have this all set up and 40 percent of your green and purple customers are leaving...you probably need to make some tweaks. But you've got to resist the urge to mess with it too often...it needs to be left alone in order to capture enough data to be useful.

At HubSpot, they would only edit the criteria every four to six months—and you might need to let it go even longer (they had over 3,000 customers at the time. Regardless, the general rule of thumb is to at least look at it quarterly. Take a SWAG. Iterate as you go.

Just like you did when you started your company in the first place.

Advocates Are Your Superheroes

Back in 2013, a Zendesk alternative called Groove conducted a small study on their users. Their CEO, Alex Turnbull, sent out an email to two groups—their power users, and a randomized "control group." The email offered their users a free month of the software if they referred one other user to Groove.

The power users sent nearly 400 percent more referrals than the other group.

Instinctively, this feels obvious. Happy customers are going to tell their friends.

It's a tried-and-true way of generating more demand from your existing customer base. But therein lies the real issue—you don't just need a bunch of customers; you need a bunch of Advocates (a.k.a. purple customers), because they're the ones that drive referrals, social proof, and more.

But you also need a system designed specifically to turn All Stars into Advocates in the first place—which is the only way to generate social proof and referrals at scale. And that's what the entire next chapter is about.

In the next chapter, you'll hear a story from the co-founders of a $10 billion SaaS company that you've definitely heard of; they'll explain how customer referrals and user-generated content were the backbones of their growth strategy. You'll also hear from a founder named Jonathan who somehow got his users to create over $100,000 of professional-grade marketing videos...for free.

5 Hot Principles

1. **Find your C.H.I.:** Build a single Customer Health Index score, just like HubSpot did, that will let you predict how likely your customers are to churn.

2. **Less is more:** Start out simple—even if it's just measuring login activity. It can evolve over time to include other important information such as key feature usage and customer satisfaction data—but don't overbuild it out of the gate.

3. **Segment your customers:** Use your C.H.I. score to segment your customers into categories—purples, greens, yellows, and reds— and build a dashboard that displays them in a clear and simple way.

4. **Drive daily actions:** Use your dashboard to drive daily actions— proactive customer outreach, offering help sessions, and sending re-engagement campaigns to customers who may have dropped off.

5. **Use the Customer Engagement Elevator™:** Work with a single goal in mind—to bring your reds up to yellow, and your yellows up to green. This simple model of progressively improving customer satisfaction will get you incredibly far. Remember... **simple solutions will scale.**

The Next Right Move

This one should be obvious—if you're not measuring a Customer Health Index for your customers, it's time to build one. If you're starting from scratch, you can just start with measuring activity—but make sure to keep it simple and focus on getting it implemented without a week's worth of work.[11]

Once you have the C.H.I. in place, pick some benchmarks to test—a number that you think will accurately segment them into green, yellow, and red categories.

You can even do this in a spreadsheet if needed—but start looking at the data and using it to prioritize your customer outreach!

Start by identifying the number 1 indicator of customer health right now:

My Number 1 customer health metric is: _____

- A Green customer would be: _____
- A Yellow customer would be: _____
- A Red customer would be: _____

---

[11] This can feel tricky – but we've got your back! Head over to softwarebook.com/health and use our worksheet to help build your C.H.I. metric (there, we've also got a video explaining how it works).

Now, go start measuring that metric and taking action on your Yellows and Reds!

CHAPTER 8

The Circle of Trust: Turning Happy Customers into Your Best Marketers

"Word of mouth is the currency of our generation."
GARY VAYNERCHUK, chairman and CEO of VaynerMedia and VaynerX
(and about fifteen other businesses)

IVAN ZHAO AND SIMON Last were less than a year into the launch of their new SaaS product, and it wasn't looking too good. They had already spent the last three years trying to find product-market fit...but it was nowhere to be found.

It was a complete mess. The two co-founders had to completely scrap the first version of their product eighteen months into development. In order to buy themselves enough runway to work on a complete rebuild, they laid off most of their team, they borrowed $150,000 from Ivan's mom to fund the work, and they moved to a small town in Japan to minimize their overhead costs.[xii]

If nothing else, they were all in. And in 2016, they launched the 2.0 version of their product.

They named it Notion. And today, it's a unicorn worth over $10 billion[xiii].

With their backs up against the wall, Ivan and Simon had been relentless in acquiring their first customers after they relaunched. They engaged in niche communities on Reddit, Hacker News, and Product Hunt. They tapped into their personal networks for intros. They guest-posted on blogs. They did literally anything they could do to get some initial traction without spending the little cash they had left. And users started to flow in...but they still didn't have enough traction to really make it.

Just as things were starting to look dire again...the two co-founders noticed a pattern that would change the course of their business forever. In particular, they noticed something about the way that their best users were spreading the word about Notion...and it was something they didn't expect.

As Camille Ricketts (Notion's co-head of marketing) put it:

> In the early days, we saw people on Twitter and Reddit sharing tips and providing support to other users. With a small marketing team, it was clear that this would be a way for us to amplify Notion.[xiv]

That insight would be the cornerstone of Notion's growth strategy—and it took them from a startup on the brink of failure in 2016 to a $2 billion valuation just two years later—and as of the writing of this book, they're sailing past 20 million active users and $100 million in revenue.

> **Their growth strategy hinged on amplifying the ways that their users were already talking about their product with their peers.**

Specifically, it included tactics like:

- Creating user communities on platforms like Reddit

- Launching template galleries for people to share and sell their Notion creations with others
- Creating an ambassador program to create massive amounts of user-generated content
- Incentivizing users to create tutorials and other assets to evangelize their product

Notion is a shining example of a company that's figured out how to help their best customers help them—and in the process, they've built an army of raving fans that are a huge growth driver, even today.

The good news? **You can run the exact same strategy by tapping into the excitement of your best customers.** And that's exactly what this chapter is all about—taking a systematic approach to making your customers the heroes of the story. And if you do this well, these heroic customers will bring you more people just like them—over and over again.

The Circle of Trust

Think about the last few significant purchases you've made—business or personal. Chances are, you looked to your peer group for signals on what decision you should make. Whether it's looking at product reviews from other customers, talking to friends or colleagues, or looking at recommendations on social media, there's a universal truth that you can't ignore:

> **Social proof is one of the most important factors in the buyer's journey.**

What do we mean by social proof? Simple—it's any type of content where the customer is the hero. And the most potent type of social proof is what we call User Generated Content (UGC)—it's content that the customers actually create themselves (testimonials, video reviews, posts in user groups or communities, etc.).

It all comes down to trust. You've got to remember, **your customers are essentially hiring your software to do a job for them.** And the question they're looking to answer is a simple one: Will your company live up to the promises you're making in the sales process? Will you be able to get the job done?

Human beings are wired to use other people's experiences in order to form an opinion—especially when it's about something they haven't yet experienced themselves. And those opinions mean the most when it's from people we already know. According to a Nielsen study, 92 percent of consumers trust recommendations from friends and family over *any* form of advertising. Think about what this means for a second:

> **There is literally nothing you can say or do that will mean more than an organic recommendation from another user.**

And the companies that figure out how to tap into this tend to grow incredibly fast. Notion was one example. Dropbox is another great one— they're famous for nailing a customer referral program using a free cloud storage offer that took them from 0 to 4 million users in their first year— and up to 400 million users by year 7[12].

If you've got a great product that people love, you probably already know how powerful it is when you get new customers via word-of-mouth referrals. They're the ones that show up already trusting you, credit card in hand, ready to speed through the demo process and get started. They're sold before the call even starts—because your customer already did the selling for you.

But despite how good that feels, founders still underestimate the financial impact of doing this at scale. Let's say every customer you

---

[12]https://timelines.issarice.com/wiki/Timeline_of_Dropbox#:~:text=Dropbox%20launches.,4%2 0omillion%20in%20January%202010.&text=Dropbox%20reaches%2050%20million%20registered,r egistered%20users%20in%20June%202015.

acquire is worth $100 per month. If one out of two customers refer another customer, and you didn't have to market to those customers, then every new customer you bring on is really worth $150 per month. Even if you have to pay sales commissions or an affiliate fee on the referral, it's still a material increase in ARPA—and one of the cheapest ways to acquire customers on earth. If every customer is worth more, that means every lead is also worth more—which means you can afford to spend more in order to acquire customers in the first place.

Fifty percent more customers than you're currently getting today from your marketing efforts? It doesn't sound too bad—but you'll like it better once you punch it into your Growth Ceiling Calculator and see how crazy the impact is.

Operationalizing this process compounds the value of all the work you're doing. Marketing, sales, product, engineering, and CS—every single area of your business becomes more efficient when your customers start referring other customers. It puts your whole funnel on steroids, and your growth becomes a self-fulfilling prophecy.

So, how do you make this flywheel of user-driven growth work for you in a predictable and repeatable way? The answer lies in something we like to call "The Win/Ask Method."

The Win/Ask Method

In 1972, in a busy shopping area in San Francisco, a humble payphone[13] stood quietly on the corner. Not too far away, Alice Isen and Paula Levin sat and watched quietly as everyday people approached the payphone to make their calls.

---

[13] Yes, we're aware that some people reading this might not be old enough to know what a payphone is. Google it ;)

One by one, they would place their call, hang up the phone, and in that exact moment...a young woman would accidentally stumble and drop a stack of papers all over the ground.

For days, Alice and Paula watched curiously as caller after caller barely glanced at the young woman and her mess, too busy with their own concerns to stop and lend a hand. By their numbers, only 4 percent of people stopped to help her—and the other 96 percent walked right past her, leaving her to struggle on her own as she chased down her papers.

These two researchers were studying human behavior [xv]– specifically, they were interested in the degree to which people are willing to go out of their way to help a stranger. And the results weren't looking too encouraging.

But the researchers had a thesis to test:

What if, right before they encountered the opportunity to be helpful, the subjects experienced something positive that lightened their mood?

Over the days that followed, they introduced a twist into the experiment. They watched closely as the next caller walked up to the phone and found an unexpected little gift from the universe in the change return slot: a shiny new dime, allegedly left behind by the caller before them.

This small discovery brought a subtle joy to the caller—and often, a little smile to their faces as well.

After the call was completed and the caller hung up the phone, the same young woman would stumble again, and the same stack of papers would once again fly all over the place—but something different was happening. The caller, touched by their own good fortune, instinctively bent down to help.

This was exactly the behavior the researchers were expecting to see more of—and things were off to a good start. However, over the next few days as more and more unwitting callers went through the same experiment, the results took a turn that nobody was expecting.

In the end, the two researchers didn't see the small increase in helpfulness that they were expecting. Instead, the difference was HUGE. How huge, you ask?

Before the dime, only 4 percent stopped to help.

And after the dime? **That number jumped to nearly 84 percent** (that's a 2,000 percent increase for all our fellow math nerds out there). Their clever experiment revealed a profound truth: Even a tiny positive moment can trigger a wave of goodwill. Or, in other words:

> ## The best time to ask someone for help is right after they win.

Unlike Alice and Paula, you don't have to camp outside for days on end watching the behavior of strangers to figure out when your customers are winning. And before you say it, you don't have to sit behind your computer and watch people's behavior to do it, either. Because you run a *software* company, you can use data to figure out the exact moments when customers are winning—and use that information to time your ask perfectly, every time.

Imagine Shopify asking for a review as soon as someone makes their first dollar online. Or Mailchimp asking for a referral once a customer reaches 1,000 email subscribers on their list. If you can identify a milestone in the customer journey that correlates to a customer winning, you also have an opportunity to ask the customer to share that win with the world.

The more wins you get them, the more trust you're building—and the more likely they are to invest even more time and effort in sharing their success on your behalf. This is the Win/Ask method—the customer wins, and you ask. And as the wins get bigger, you can ask them to go deeper in what they share—building a systematic process for generating social proof, word-of-mouth marketing, and direct referrals.

Our framework for building this system is called the Customer Value Chain™—and it's something that every single SaaS company on Earth can benefit from.

The Customer Value Chain™

The idea of the Customer Value Chain™ is pretty simple—at each link of the chain, as the customer grows more and more attached to your company and your product, you can make an increasingly larger request for their energy to help find more customers just like them. The Customer Value Chain™ starts by asking for some simple soundbites, and then progresses over time to more advanced moves, like co-hosting a webinar or inviting them to share a stage at your next event.

With the proper systems in place, you'll be able to re-engage with your customer at each stage of the Customer Value Chain™—and the best part is that this approach works at scale.

The Customer Value Chain

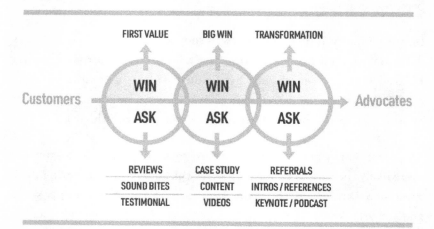

The goal is simple. You want to take your All-Star customers (which you learned about in the last chapter) and turn them into Advocates at specific milestones—for instance, if they give you a great NPS score, generate a certain amount of revenue using your platform, or achieve a specific ROI threshold. Once they hit the milestone, you engage with them and celebrate—by telling the world about their success.

As you can see in the model above, we break the Customer Value Chain™ into three stages—with the "ask" at each stage getting progressively deeper. Ideally, you can jot down three sequential "wins" that a customer will experience in your platform—each one representing a higher degree of success than the one before it. Once you have that, you can tie each "win" to a stage of the Customer Value Chain™.

Oh, and there's one extra benefit of turning All Stars into Advocates—your "purple customers" are the least likely to churn out of anyone. Why? Because you've "anointed" them. You've made them part of something special. The inner circle. The trusted crew. The top 1 percent of customers. And what's even better is that they've announced it publicly. Building a strong group of Advocates is the most advanced strategy you can run in order to bullet-proof your retention. And this framework will show you exactly how to do it.

Stage 1: Reviews and User-Generated Content

The first level of "ask" is a quick and easy way for your customers to spread the word about you—and in some cases, it might not require any time from them at all.

> **When someone experiences their first big win on your platform, hit them with a simple ask to leave you a review or to write a short testimonial.**

Think of ways to make this as easy as possible. If your ask is for a review, give them the direct links to the specific page. And if it's a written testimonial, you can even pre-write a blurb based on their data and ask them for approval (your busiest customers will be thankful for the help).

This ask doesn't have to be the same for every customer—you can adjust it based on your needs. For instance, if you have enough website testimonials but could use some more Capterra reviews, that's what you should ask for. Just direct the social proof towards the next place where you want to build authority.

> ## This first stage is about generating a high volume of social proof.

You'll go deeper in the next couple of stages, but the goal here is to keep the time investment to a minimum for your customer—especially because you should be running this play on their "first big win." As long as you keep them winning, you earn the right to keep going deeper and raising the quality bar in the future.

Stage 2: Case Studies and Customer Content

Recently, we caught up with Jonathan Pototschnik, one of the co-founders of Service Autopilot, which is an all-in-one SaaS platform for lawncare and home service businesses. Jonathan is an incredible founder with all-around great ideas—but one of the most innovative strategies that he introduced into his business was the Service Autopilot Academy—a coaching program that was designed entirely to help his ideal customers grow their businesses.

There's lots to learn from his Academy strategy, but our favorite part is what he called the Biggest Badass Competition. This competition was a pure stroke of genius—he was able to get his best customers to create hundreds of powerful, professional-quality videos about the impact his company had on their lives...essentially for free.

Here's how it worked: Jonathan and his team launched a contest to all his customers and promised a $10,000 trip to Italy for them and their families as the top prize. All they had to do in order to enter was shoot an eight- to twelve-minute video documenting their personal transformations (that happened as a result of their relationship with Service Autopilot).

They coached their clients on what made a great video—length, content, how to make it dramatic and tell a great story...the whole nine yards. Jonathan's team watched the videos, whittled them down, and voted on the top three. And here's where it gets even cooler:

> ## At their annual customer conference, they played the top 3 videos—and the crowd voted for a winner.

This idea was genius for a couple reasons. First, the winner got an all-expenses paid trip, which reinforced the values that Jonathan and his team were instilling in the first place. And the second? You guessed it:

> It was a built-in sales tool. We took these videos and made them part of our marketing, part of our sales process, and part of our onboarding—and they did a great job showing the market that our software was a better option than anything else out there.

This strategy was crucial to Service Autopilot's s success. As one of the only bootstrapped companies in its space, the team was constantly competing against heavily funded competitors who could outspend them on engineering, marketing, and customer success. But this user generated content was a massive differentiator that helped build trust in the market—in an authentic way that none of their big, venture-funded competitors could manage to pull off. These videos would have cost him multiple six figures to produce on his own. Instead, he got them all for the price of a fancy vacation.

Jonathan's business is yet another example of a small startup that experienced meteoric growth on the back of customer-driven marketing strategies. Service Autopilot was entirely bootstrapped and sold for over nine figures in 2019. Jonathan's journey from zero to sold is an amazing success story by every possible measure.

These customer-produced videos are just one of many examples of the types of content we can create at Stage 2 of the Customer Value Chain™. Our big goal here is to make the customer the hero of the story and put them at the center of a case study, video, podcast episode, webinar, or any other medium that lets them share their win with the world.

When this is done right, your customers will be thanking you for the opportunity.

We do this at SaaS Academy all the time—we love bringing founders on stage to share "Ten Minute Tactics" about what's working in their business—especially when they're having massive growth and hitting goals. We also run "hot seats" after our clients exit their businesses so they can share lessons learned.

> **When customers win big, get them to share their story. Your product might just happen to be an important character in that story.**

There's one big challenge with this type of content: your clients aren't always great storytellers.

The 3S Testimonial Template™

A lot of people don't know what to say the minute a camera turns on. Even for people who seem outgoing or extroverted, putting them in the spotlight can lock 'em right up.

But if you want to nail your user-generated content strategy, it's got to be good—which means you'll need to coach them. Just like Jonathan gave his clients some tips on how to create a great video, you should do the same thing—and our favorite framework for this is called the 3S Testimonial Template™ (you can head over to softwarebook.com/ask to download a template and some examples).

1.   **Situation:** Describe the scene at the beginning of the story. Specifics help here—dates, revenue levels, names, and emotions will all help paint a great starting point.

2.   **Struggle:** Every great story is built on the pain of a struggle against a worthy adversary. Make sure that your customer pushes hard on this—they should go deep into the pain that they were experiencing before they had their "win" with your software.

3.   **Solution:** Coach your customer to always include the answer that helped them solve the pain. As we like to say, every "win" should come with a "how" alongside it.

Here's an example:

We started Centsical in 2015 because we realized that most early-stage SaaS founders didn't have the money or the know-how to do financial forecasting. After a few years of struggling, we really hit our stride in 2018 and have grown to over $30 million in revenue.

Once we hit around 100 employees, dealing with HR-related issues became a huge problem. We had misalignment across the company around hiring and firing practices, our talent acquisition was slow and inconsistent, and we had a ton of vulnerability around employment-related lawsuits.

That's when we found Hirely. Once we implemented their software and signed up for their fractional People Ops service, we were able to create SOPs around hiring, firing, and performance management. Our average time to fill a role decreased from 60 days to under 41, our employee NPS has increased from +12 to +48, and our legal exposure is much smaller thanks to all of their help and expertise. We've saved over $80,000 in legal bills compared to last year—the ROI is super clear for us.

For most companies, this is a natural progression from Stage 1 of the Customer Value Chain™. Not every customer will make it to Stage 2, but if you look at your happiest and most engaged customers, you can double-down by inviting them on stage at events, recording podcast episodes with them, or other ways to promote them in a positive light.

For most customers, this will be an incredibly positive experience—and one that'll endear you to your customer forever.

Stage 3: Referrals and References

After you've gotten some solid social proof and case study material from your customers, it's time to move them up to the highest level—referrals, references, and other high-value asks. While these may organically happen earlier in the process, the systematic action in this stage is the most potent ingredient in the Customer Value Chain™—it's the one that will directly drive growth for your company.

At this stage, you're explicitly asking your customer to reach into their network and lend you the trust that they've built with someone they know. This might show up as an open-ended ask for them to refer people who your software can help, or coming to them with a specific ask for someone you already know they're connected with.

Specifically in enterprise sales, this can also manifest as a sales reference or an ask for an introduction to members of leadership in another business unit or team as a way to expand your product into new areas. You might also find yourself making "high effort" asks such as appearing on a podcast, joining a customer advisory board, speaking at a customer event, or leading a user group.

Whatever it looks like, there's one universal truth:

Making a top-level ask requires a lot of trust.

So, with that in mind, the most important decision you'll make is *when* to make the ask. And the answer is pretty simple: right after they say something nice about you.

You can't just expect referrals to happen automatically. Just like in sales, you've got to *ask for the deal*. In his famous book, *Influence: The Psychology of Persuasion*, Robert Cialdini calls this the Principle of Commitment and Consistency. The principle is simple: once people commit to something verbally or in writing, they're significantly more likely to follow through on what they said they would do.

The act of asking for a referral is simple—it's everything leading up to the ask that's harder to pull off. At Stage 3 of the Customer Value Chain™, think of everything that's already happened:

- You've talked to the customer via your marketing channels and your funnel
- You've had a sales conversation, asked for the deal, and gotten it
- You've onboarded the customer, ensuring that they've reached First Value quickly
- You've measured their success with the platform, and have a good sense that they're happy and receiving value

- You've seen at least three significant "wins" or ROI moments since they've been your customer, and you've likely already asked for some sort of social proof or case study material.

Just like in sports, the referral game is won or lost before it starts. Everything in this entire book so far has led up to this moment—being able to ask a customer for referrals and having them say yes, without hesitation.

And when you get there...it's an incredible feeling (and an incredible growth lever, too).

Personalized Outreach Can Still Scale

If you're thinking that this all makes sense but sounds like a lot to manage...well, you're right. In order to drive serious results from this strategy, you've got to have a system to capture wins at certain milestones so you can celebrate them with your customers.

> **For every major milestone, you should systematize or automate the "ask" that comes next.**

Automation is the best way to make sure that you're capturing social proof consistently. For example, at UpLaunch, Matt sent an email to every client once they'd captured their first fifty leads through their software. That email also went out to the customer success team so they could use it to start up a personalized conversation. They also had an automation that tracked when customers submitted a 10 out of 10 NPS score and triggered an email introduction to their marketing team, where they'd ask to produce a case study on the customer.

Capturing the wins is the foundation of this whole system—nothing can really happen without it. It's so easy to not celebrate wins without a system, simply because your happiest customers are usually not the ones who are sending in support tickets and asking tons of questions. A great way to solve this is by incentivizing your customer success team around social-proof-creation. For instance, Johnny's team at Silvertrac was expected to generate twelve reviews and one case study every quarter. It was simply part of their role, and they made it happen.

Marcel says it like this: "Your product is Yoda, and your customers are Luke Skywalker." Sometimes, your customers don't even realize they're making progress—and you have to tell them. Send them a message when they crush that sales goal, or capture those first hundred leads—whatever the mission of your software is, you've got to remind your customers when they achieve it.

Yoda, you must be. To help them celebrate, your job is.

Building A Machine to Extract Customer Value

There are a few key ingredients to building a machine that captures wins which you can turn into social proof, case studies, and referrals:

1. **Seed the Request:** It's a great practice to tell your clients up front (during sales or onboarding) that you're going to ask for a case study or referral after you've delivered the results that you've promised.

2. **Measure Client Wins:** Define the signals that show you when customers are winning so you can build systems and automation around those milestones.

3. **Automate the Ask:** Architect the "next step" after every category of wins and automate some sort of handoff or notification so that your team knows exactly what to expect.

4. **Focus on Distribution:** Especially at the first two stages of the Customer Value Chain™, the strategy will be most effective if the customer sees themselves getting promoted in your marketing and in front of other customers. Close the loop with the customer and show them where to find their social proof in the wild.

5. **Do It on Repeat:** Just like delivering value to your customers—this is a process, not an event. Keep the machine running and work to generate social proof at scale.

This chapter is the culmination of a lot of hard work for any high-performing SaaS company. Driving referrals at scale from your customer base is incredibly powerful—when done right, it'll be your lowest cost marketing channel, your highest-impact activity for building a strong brand, and a way to showcase your raving fans and truly create a movement in your market.

But like we said before, there's a lot that goes into it. You've got to nail your marketing, sales, activation, and retention in order to pull this off. But once you do, as long as you have customers, you'll be able to multiply them by following the simple steps in this chapter.

There's still one element we haven't talked about yet, and it's a big one. It's so big, in fact, that getting it wrong can completely flatline your growth, even if you do everything else right. This key element is pricing.

In the next chapter, you'll meet a founder who undercharged his customers for years. And when he finally stopped, the end result was nothing short of incredible.

5 Hot Principles

1. **Your customers are your best salespeople:** There's nothing more credible, trusted and potent as a customer winning with your product telling their friends about how awesome you are.

2. **Don't leave WOM to chance:** Most companies let word-of-mouth marketing happen organically, but if you really want to grow fast, help your customers share their wins and amplify their message in a systematic way.

3. **The win/ask method:** Your customers are significantly more likely to say yes to an ask—and say something nice about you—right after they've gotten a win with your product. Start tracking these moments so you can perfectly time a helpful suggestion to spread the word.

4. **One step at a time:** Use the Customer Value Chain™ to identify increasingly meaningful wins in your customer's journey, and pair it with increasingly potent asks for social proof, user-generated content, and referrals.

5. **Simple stories sell:** Use the 3S Testimonial Template™ to help your customers share their story in a clear and compelling way that will actually drive engagement.

The Next Right Move

Head over to softwarebook.com/ask and snag all of our resources. We've got a worksheet to help you architect your win/ask moments, as well as an editable version of the 3S Testimonial Template™ (with some extra tweaks to make it even better).

Once you're armed with the resources, it's time to commit to some fast action. Think of the first moment in your customer's journey where they achieve a win—ideally one that they came looking for when they signed up for your product.

My customer's first win: _____

Now, write down the first "ask" that you'll make (from Stage 1 of the Customer Value Chain™) when that win is achieved.

My   first   ask   will   be:
_____

Once you've identified that moment, start tracking every user that achieves the milestone and make the ask as soon as you see it happen. Even if you have to do it manually right now, *start today*—and build the machine later.

EXPANSION—Make Customers More Valuable

CHAPTER 9

How to Build the Pricing Plan You Actually Deserve

"Pricing fundamentally determines the nature of the product *
and the structure of the business that produces it."
JASON COHEN, founder of WP Engine

SIMPLECONSIGN, A B2B SaaS platform that helps consignment shops streamline their point-of-sale and back-office operations, is a pretty niche offering (clearly). The founder, Joe Gaboury, was a SaaS Academy client for years—and is a great example of a founder who is fiercely loyal to his customers.

When Joe first started SimpleConsign, he was determined to not be like "all those big companies" that raised prices every year just to carve out an extra percentage point on their bottom lines. And for a while, he succeeded—he went multiple years without adjusting pricing, and scaled SimpleConsign to about $2 million in annual revenue.

Despite this growth, he was running into a Growth Ceiling of his own. In that time, the product had changed massively—and it took a lot to keep it running, growing, and innovating. But his pricing hadn't changed along with the product. . . and he had to make a choice between pivoting outside of his small market to grow. . . or adjusting his pricing.

He realized that he was charging way too little for the value that he was providing—and when he finally changed his pricing structure, he added almost $750,000 to his revenue immediately—which unlocked his ability to continue to invest in the product improvements that his niche customer base so desperately wanted.

But that's not even the crazy part. Joe, like any founder who hasn't raised prices before, was super nervous about how his customers would react. But if you talk to any founder who's been through this and come out the other side, they'll tell you that we make it worse in our heads than it is in real life. As Joe puts it, "I just grabbed the bull by the horns. I made the changes that we needed to make, sent the email from my own email account, and put my cell number on the bottom."

The end result? SimpleConsign only lost one customer as a result of the price increase (who came back a month or two later).

In many situations, the result that we desire is just on the other side of the thing we fear the most. But for many founders, they're not sure exactly how to get past the fear and get their pricing adjusted.

Our answer? Math (predictably).

Joe is a smart founder—he knew his "break even" number[14]—in other words, that he could lose about 27 percent of his customer base after the price increase and still break even. And since he was reasonably sure that wouldn't happen, it gave him the confidence he needed to make the decision. It was time to capture more of the value he'd been creating and move his business forward.

---

[14] If you want a downloadable "break even" calculator, just head over to softwarebook.com/pricing where we've got one you can snag for free.

Here's the bottom line: if you're reading this, you should probably raise your prices. Yes, you may lose a few customers—but once you do the math, you'll see the truth: your business will be way better off losing a few customers if you're making more from those who stay. As Dan always says, "If nobody's telling you 'no,' you need to raise your prices."

> **Charging more money and saying goodbye to a few customers is better than not charging enough and seeing your business die a slow death.**

This is probably the number-one issue that we see with first-time founders. It's also why SaaS pricing has its own group of experts—of which our friend Marcos Rivera is one of the best. He literally wrote a book on the topic called *Street Pricing*—and much of this chapter is inspired by his genius brain and some of the guest sessions he did inside of SaaS Academy.

***

> **"If someone bought your business tomorrow, what's the first thing you think they would do?"**

When we ask that question to founders, the vast majority of them say that it would be a price raise. And if that's you, don't worry. We've been there before, we know how you probably got there, too, and, most importantly, we know how to fix it.

Here's our guess on how you picked your first pricing structure:

You hopped on Google. You looked at how your competition was priced (even though they don't quite do exactly what you do). Then, you compared your features to theirs (even though they don't directly match up). From there, you ballparked a number, probably reduced it by 20 percent, and voila—pricing appears.

Over time, you probably added "levels"—an entry-level plan that was maybe 30 percent less than your original, and a pro-level plan that was 30 percent higher. You rolled it out, took a huge sigh of relief, crossed your fingers that you wouldn't have to mess with it for a while, and got back to building.

We get it—that's how almost every founder starts—just like in chapter 7, when we talked about using a SWAG (Scientific Wild-Ass Guess) for your first attempt at a Customer Health Index, you probably used it for your first pricing plan. It's not 100 percent bad to start this way. . . but now that you've got this book, it's time to apply some science to your pricing.

So yes, you probably should raise your prices. But before you do it, we're going to unpack a method for creating a pricing structure that you'll feel great about. It'll make sure that you're not leaving a crazy amount of money on the table (like Joe was), and that you'll feel comfortable charging more money when your customer gets more value.

In other words, we want you to have a strong foundational understanding of how to set up your pricing structure, and the right ways to tweak it over time. That's what we'll cover here in this chapter—and then in the next one, we'll go deep on exactly how to execute the price increase when the time comes.

The Pricing Triangle

Pricing can be tricky—especially if you feel like you just randomly assigned some dollars to your product in the early days. Are you charging too much? Too little? SaaS products are inherently difficult to price—because most of your costs take place up front. Your fixed costs such as development generally need to happen to get the platform built in the first place, and your variable costs (sales, marketing, and implementation) are generally the highest as we're driving towards the sale and in the few months immediately afterwards. Because of that, here's the first thing about pricing we really need to drive home:

> ## Profits are driven by serving a higher number of customers for a longer period of time.

This might feel obvious, but it's super important to remember it as we work through your pricing structure in this chapter. If you're selling movie tickets or cups of lemonade, you're generally "covering costs"—each transaction stands on its own. SaaS can capitalize big-time on economy of scale, because there's not as much incremental cost for servicing new customers, especially once they've been on board for a few months. It's why we focus so much on acquisition and activation—they're the hurdles that you need to clear in order to run a durable (and profitable) business.

But without the right pricing structure, it's all for nothing. You can do everything right and still not make enough money to keep the business afloat. And while there are plenty of articles and frameworks out there about pricing, our favorite one comes from the brain of an incredible SaaS founder and investor named David Skok.

David is a four-time founder with three IPOs. Yes, really. Nowadays, he is a venture capitalist at Matrix Partners (and writes on his legendary blog, www.forentrepreneurs.com). David has written extensively about a simple, three-level pricing model that can help any SaaS business develop a clear pricing strategy—and the data we've seen Marcos share in his training sessions backs it up. By borrowing heavily from these two pricing visionaries, we've boiled it all down to a simple method that almost every founder can implement: The Pricing Triangle.

The Pricing Triangle

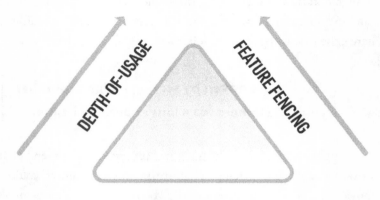

VALUE METRIC

Let's start with the foundation of the triangle (and of your pricing strategy): the Value Metric.

> **Value Metric: the one key result that's driving value for the majority of your customers.**

Getting this right is the first big unlock. As Patrick Cambell (co-founder of ProfitWell) says, "If you get your Value Metric right, you can get a lot of other things wrong and still be alright." It's that critical—but there's also some nuance to getting this right. If you anchor too hard on your Value Metric as the only price driver, you can actually make your users want to use your product *less* (more on this in a bit).

The second element to the Pricing Triangle is depth-of-usage—this one comes right out of David's playbook.

> **Depth-of-usage driver: a secondary metric that is likely to increase when overall value delivery also increases, but is *not* the primary Value Metric.**

Setting up a few depth-of-usage drivers is a great strategy to drive upgrades or implement usage-based pricing—*especially* if your primary Value Metric might not cover all the angles. Examples of this include having pricing drivers based on things like number of API calls, database size, number of contacts, etc.

Pricing based on depth-of-usage is super common in CRMs, content management platforms, and learning management solutions as well. Andrew Ferraccioli, the CEO of a learning management platform called Searchie, has a great example of this. Searchie is wild—they've built some incredibly deep AI functionality into a traditional LMS / video hosting platform—and they roll it all up into a feature called a Hub. On their lowest pricing plan, you get one "Hub" of content...and as you need additional Hubs, you move up the plan stack.

However, they've also implemented a depth-of-usage driver based on "hours of video storage"—which the user can upgrade as an add-on, or drive them to upgrade to the next plan level (which of course has more storage included). This way, even if a customer only has one hub that they're using to serve a ton of videos, Searchie can still adjust their pricing plan to match the value they're delivering.

The last element to the Pricing Triangle is *feature fencing*.

> **Feature fencing: offering specific features only on certain plan levels in order to drive upgrades between plans.**

Power users will need functionality that other users won't need, and a great pricing plan will make sure that you're driving those power users to the plan that makes sense. Take Gusto for instance—it's a US-based HR and payroll platform led by CEO and co-founder Josh Reeves. Although they do a lot of marketing towards small startups who want to run payroll without a ton of headaches, if you look at their high-end plan, they've got a LOT there: cost-center group budgets, third-party plugins, and an advanced reporting suite.

Are those critical for most users who want to just do something that's easier and safer than writing paper checks? Nope. But as Gusto's customers evolve and grow their businesses, Gusto's plan levels and feature fencing strategies allow them to grow side by side—which is exactly what you want to do, too.

That covers a high-level overview of the triangle, but in order to do this justice, we're going to give you a breakdown of each part—because when done right, this is the most important decision you can make in your SaaS company. We've also got a ton of resources to help you build a world-class pricing plan at softwarebook.com/pricing, including calculators, pricing teardowns, and more.

The Value Metric

Let's take a look at a SaaS company everybody knows: Netflix. If you had to guess, what would their Value Metric be?

We don't know for sure, but we'd guess it's probably something like hours of content viewed per account per month or something similar. Their goal is to get people to watch their content—simple as that. But imagine for a minute if Netflix just did a straight pricing driver on this Value Metric. How would user behavior change? Would "binge watching" still be a thing? Would TV producers still want to release entire seasons at once? If users were restricted by their plan levels and couldn't watch the content they wanted, there's a good chance they'd just watch less Netflix.

So instead, Netflix uses other dimensions to drive pricing. From a depth-of-usage standpoint, they priced according to the numbers of users on the account (and later, switched to the number of devices on the account since everyone was just sharing their passwords). They also leverage feature fencing for things like HD viewing, downloading episodes, and enabling spatial audio.

Netflix is a great example of a pricing strategy that relies on all sides of the triangle. They have a clear Value Metric (hours of content viewed) and are using all of the other strategies we mentioned to drive ascension as an account's Value Metric increases.

> **Ascension is the movement of a customer from their current plan level to a higher-priced one.**

What makes a great Value Metric? Ideally, you're tying *your* Value Metric to the growth of your *customer's* company. That way, they'll see their own success and attribute at least some of it to using your product (or justify the increased price as a "cost of their growth"). Highlighting the correlation between your product and their growth will make it much easier to expand their value over time.

It might feel tough to figure this out—but it's worth it. Remember Patrick Campbell from earlier? He's done an incredible amount of research on SaaS pricing—and his data shows that **the companies who build their pricing around a Value Metric grow at double the rate compared to those who only use features** to differentiate between plans.

This is why this "third lever"—**Making Customers More Valuable**—is so potent. Yes, you need to Get More Customers, and yes, you need to Keep Customers Longer. But it gets *much* easier to hit a revenue goal when your customers are steadily getting more valuable over time.

10x Value

Let's say you're earning $5,000 per account per year in your company. If you got an offer to add another client for a cost of only $500, would you take it?

Of course you would. You'd make $4,500 off of that client—it's nearly a 10x return.

That experience is exactly how your customers should feel.

> **Your customers should be getting a 10x return on their investment in your SaaS platform.**

That probably sounds intimidating, or hard to track—and that's okay. You might have to do some digging to figure out the extra revenue that your solution is generating for a customer. But that is a fundamental product skill of a B2B SaaS company—you should be able to work with a customer to assign a rough dollar value to your Value Metric, which will in turn, help inform your pricing strategy.

For example, in Matt's first company UpLaunch, they knew their customer's numbers cold. They had data on the price of an average membership for the types of gyms that their customers ran and knew that if they could get them just two new members, they'd more than "cover the cost" of the subscription—and by the time they'd helped the gym get twelve, they were approaching "10x return" territory.

This knowledge informed everything from pricing strategy to the way that they onboarded customers—for instance, they ran a specific marketing strategy for their client gyms that was extremely likely to generate those first two new members within the first thirty days because they knew that if they got the costs covered before the second bill hit, the customers were much more likely to stick around long term.

Take a good, long look at your client's business. What new revenue are you helping them bring in? Are you helping them acquire customers or retain customers longer? Are you introducing efficiencies that might save them from having to make a hire? Or recovering cash that they otherwise would lose?

Whatever it is that you're helping them do, strive as hard as you can to provide a 10x return on what you're charging them—it makes sales easier, holds your product development to a very high standard, and makes sure that you know your customers incredibly well—all of which are good things for your company.

Don't Disincentivize

We talked about this a little bit in the Netflix example, but it's worth restating: if you build a one-dimensional pricing plan that's only based on your Value Metric, you risk disincentivizing your users. Or to say it more simply:

> **If you charge your users based on how much they use your product, they might just decide to use your product less.**

When Marcos taught this in SaaS Academy, he used Slack as an example:

Slack's Value Metric is probably "number of messages sent." It's the atomic unit of using Slack—you've got to send messages in a workspace in order to get any sort of value out of the platform whatsoever.

But does Slack charge people based on how many messages they send? Nope—if they did, every time a user sent a message, they'd likely pause and ask, "is it worth it?" Or in larger organizations, they'd probably have managers asking their teams to not communicate in Slack so they don't hit a certain billing threshold—taking the actual behaviors in the opposite direction from what they want from a product standpoint.

If you're old enough to remember waiting until 7 p.m. to call someone on your cell phone, you know exactly what we're talking about. And if you aren't...here's the deal: cell phone companies used to include a fixed number of minutes in their monthly plans—but would include "free nights and weekends" as a bonus. And our behaviors followed suit—we'd simply *call people less* until we hit the 7 p.m. threshold for "free nights," and then start using the hell out of it after that. And yes, this was before text messages were a thing...but that's another conversation.

Bottom line: this is why we love building pricing drivers that are based on *depth-of-usage*—it generates a similar result without making your users want to stop using your product. How does Slack do this? They start with a free tier that includes *unlimited messaging* (which is their actual Value Metric)—but they cap the number of integrations and only let you see messages that were sent within the past 90 days. Why? Because once a user has used Slack with their team for three months, connected it to a few other apps, and sent thousands of messages, it's part of their daily workflow. And they *know* that sooner or later, a user will need to look back in their message history further than 90 days—which will drive the upgrade.

The most ninja part of it all? Slack doesn't *delete* the messages...they keep the history, and only unlock it for people on the paid plan—so you can literally upgrade to get access to your message history. Stewart Butterfield (Slack's founder and former CEO) said in an interview that *search* is one of their most important features...so building a depth-of-usage driver around message history (which is what their users are searching through) is a genius move.

Looking at these two examples, what are the key differences between how old cell phone plans worked and how Slack works today? It's simple: Slack has built their pricing in a way that it doesn't restrict your usage directly—it helps you get hooked on the product, doesn't directly stand in the way of your ability to get value from the product...and then once you're past the point of no return, you "bump into a limit" and end up needing to upgrade.

If that sounds exciting to you, the first step is nailing the Value Metric itself—because without that, you won't know the behavior you're trying to incentivize. Marcos asks a series of six questions to evaluate whether or not your Value Metric is strong:

1. Does the metric grow with increased usage of the platform?
2. Is it easy to track?
3. Is it easy for your customer to understand?
4. Can the customer predict their budget / usage ahead of time?
5. Does the customer perceive it as fair?
6. Does the metric tend to grow when the customer's business also grows?

If you can answer "yes" to all of these, your Value Metric is probably solid.

Depth-of-Usage

Omar Zenhom is the co-founder of WebinarNinja, an all-in-one webinar platform for coaches. He's developed an incredible pricing model for his product—and it's primarily driven by picking the right depth-of-usage drivers.

His pricing page has the typical "good-better-best" plan levels, but there's also a slider right above the plans—which you can adjust based on your audience size—and the pricing automatically updates on-screen.

We love this for two reasons—one, "number of attendees on your webinar" is probably the key Value Metric for his customers, and he pulls it forward and uses it to drive pricing. In his case, it won't disincentivize users because there's revenue tied to webinar attendees—it's an outstanding Value Metric, and it grows alongside his customer's businesses.

But the other part below the surface? There are *additional* depth-of-usage drivers baked into his plan limits, outside of the number of attendees, which will also drive upgrades—in his case, it's length of time per webinar and number of users on the account. They're likely driving a meaningful amount of ascension between plans, but since they're not the core Value Metric (and likely wouldn't pass Marcos' six question test as well as "number of attendees"), they're not featured as prominently on the pricing page.

The point here is that there are likely features in *your* software that should be priced based on depth-of-usage. And if you're not sure...here's how to tell:

> **If a feature will drive value for *all* plan levels, and increased usage probably equates to increased value for the customer...you should consider using it as a "depth-of-usage" driver.**

For your platform, maybe it's API calls, database size, storage room, number of users per account, or something else entirely. Don't overthink it—as long as you're figuring out the components "under the hood" that will keep users on the appropriate plan level as their business grows, you'll be in a good place.

Feature Fencing

Leveraging additional features to drive your pricing model might feel obvious. As the price increases, so does the functionality. But like most things, there are some important nuances to doing this right.

There are two main ways to "fence" a feature in SaaS. The first one is by using your various plan levels—for instance, the Pro plan will include features that the Starter plan doesn't include. The second way is to pull the feature out of all of the plans, and instead sell it as an add-on.

Our most common question from founders when we talk about add-ons: "Why not just include them in our highest plan level and call it a day?"

The answer to that question has little to do with your P&L, and a lot to do with human psychology. Most humans feel allergic to waste—specifically if they feel like they're wasting their money. So, if you take the "easy way out" and just toss a whole bunch of features into your top plan—and half of them are irrelevant to the majority of your customers—you'll actually *hurt* your customer retention.

> ## Customers will churn if they feel like they're paying for something they're not using.

Our friend Trevor Mauch, the CEO of Carrot, shared his story of when he went through this. His company provides lead generation and CRMs for real estate investors and had historically been priced with the standard "three plan" model, which drove significant expansion revenue for years.

But as the team continued to add features to their higher end plans, he noticed that expansion revenue was getting flatter and flatter—and he wasn't sure why. After digging into his product usage data, he found that there were multiple features on his top-level plan that were being used by less than *thirty percent of their customers*. He explained it like this: "The people who were using them were valuing them highly—but in order to use them, they had to go from $99 per month up to $200 per month—and the overall value just wasn't there."

Trevor and his team re-worked Carrot's pricing model to break out these features into "suites," which can be added to any of their regular plans—

and took this opportunity to re-work the plans and price points at the same time. After some tweaking and tuning, their expansion revenue is once again outpacing their churn, the right customers are using the right features, and their overall ARPA has gone from $116 per month to $130 per month—*an average 12 percent increase on the value of every one of their customers.*

Bundling too many features into a pricing plan might feel like a good move at the time—but it can actually hurt your expansion revenue *and* negatively impact retention. Think about it—if you add features that people *don't need* into a pricing plan, the customers on that plan will feel like they're not making good use of what they're paying for—and that will show up in your numbers, guaranteed.

If a feature would be valuable for the majority of your user base, it should be priced into a regular plan. But in the words of Marcos...

> ## "Ideal add-ons create a <u>lot</u> of value for a <u>few</u> of your customers."

These might be things like custom integrations, premium services, advanced analytics and reporting, or specific security audits. An added bonus of charging for add-ons is that it lets you say *yes* to features that carry a variable cost—because you'll have a way to offset it. We're going to go *deep* on these in chapter 11—because when they're done right, services and other add-ons are an incredible driver to **Make Customers More Valuable** (and more successful, too).

Roll It All into One

Once you put together all three sides of the triangle—your Value Metric, some depth-of-usage drivers, and some strategic feature fencing—you've got all the ingredients of a comprehensive pricing model. With this solid foundation, you can iterate on your plan levels and the thresholds between them in order to maximize your average revenue per account.

The goal, of course, is to move your users up the plan levels—but the most common question we get from founders is "how many"? The majority of founders tend to set very loose plan thresholds, and then also charge too little to begin with—resulting in a business that requires a ton of work for a fraction of the revenue it could be generating.

But we know you want specifics—and we've got 'em. Or more specifically, Marcos has 'em. If you're wondering how long each user should stay at each plan level (as a benchmark), here's what he coaches:

- **60 in 6:** 60% of accounts in the lowest level plan should hit their plan limits in 6-9 months

- **40 in 8:** 40% of accounts in the middle level plan should hit their plan limits in 8-12 months

- **20 in 12:** 20% of accounts in the top-level plan should hit their plan limits in 12-18 months

Ideally, your pricing plan will be built (using the triangle we just taught you) so that you can continue to increase customer value when these plan limits are hit (either via usage-based charges or by moving up to the next plan).

When it comes to determining what to include in each plan, our friend Bill Wilson (two-time founder and SaaS pricing expert) has a simple framework for thinking about it:

"Each plan should be designed to solve a problem or do a job your customer is hiring your product to do."

Specifically, here's what you need to figure out in order to build a pricing plan that'll be the foundation of your growth for years to come:

1.   A clear Value Metric that passes Marcos' six-question test with flying colors

2.   A short list of other metrics that will increase as the customer gets more value—these are potential candidates for depth-of-usage drivers

3.   A list of your key features, and which plan level you think they should correlate to, based on the problem your customer is solving.

From there, you can draft up three plan levels, figure out some thresholds for your depth-of-usage metrics, and list which features belong in which plan. In a perfect world, you'd be able to pull some usage data around these items—but you know what we're going to say next: if you're not sure, take a SWAG and run a test—*for new customers only*.

This is a big idea—you should experiment with your pricing structure frequently (and you'll learn exactly how to do it in the next chapter). And once you land on a structure that works...you can move your *existing* customers onto the new structure and you're off to the races.

That last part—changing prices for your existing customers—intimidates a disproportionate number of founders. And if you read this chapter and were like "okay, I've got to rebuild my pricing —but how the heck do I roll it out without getting crushed by churn?"—the next chapter is exactly what you're asking for.

We're going to teach you the best way to deploy a price increase...without getting demolished by a tsunami of angry customers. It's backed by data. It's been successfully executed hundreds of times. And by the end of the next chapter, you'll know exactly how to do it (email templates included).

5 Hot Principles

1. **Pricing is a huge lever:** Don't underestimate the financial impact that fixing your pricing will have on your business. A great business with a bad price will still ultimately fail. If this is the "one thing" you've been procrastinating on, it's time to stop.

2. **Use the Pricing Triangle:** Great pricing consists of three key ingredients: a Value Metric, depth-of-usage drivers, and feature fencing. Use all three to craft pricing models that encourage usage, and organically increase price as customers unlock more and more value from your platform.

3. **Create a strong metric:** Identify the key metric that maps to the value your customers get. It should be easy to track and understand, perceived as fair and correlate with the growth of your customer's business. A strong Value Metric helps tie your product's success to your customer's success.

4. **Remember depth-of-usage and feature fencing:** Segment features and usage thresholds into higher tier plans to further align your pricing and packaging to value without disincentivizing usage in the immediate term. Features that create significant value for a small number of users but don't correlate to your plan tiers can be split out as add-ons.

5. **Know your breakeven point:** Understanding the breakeven point is crucial when considering a price increase. Joe knew he could lose up to 27 percent of his customers and still break even, which gave him the confidence to proceed with the price adjustment (more on that in the next chapter).

The Next Right Move

Armed with the Pricing Triangle, we're going to run a few exercises to help you build a pricing plan that can truly support your revenue growth.

Review the Value Metric section and come up with your own Value Metric and make sure it passes the six-question test that Marcos has created.

My Value Metric is: _____

Next, come up with at least three other ideas for depth-of-usage drivers. As a reminder, these are metrics that will grow as your customer gets more value from your software, but they are *not* your primary Value Metric. These secondary metrics should help to drive additional revenue via usage-based pricing and/or upgrades.

Driver #1: _____

Driver #2: _____

Driver #3: _____

Last but not least, head over to softwarebook.com/pricing and check out our Feature Fencing Quadrant™—which will help you decide which features to include in your plan levels and which ones to package as add-ons.

Once you've completed those three steps, you should have all of the ingredients of an elite pricing plan. If you want to see some teardowns of how other SaaS companies assemble these ingredients into a plan that truly scales, softwarebook.com/pricing has everything you need.

CHAPTER 10

The Ultimate Price-Increase Method™

*"You can determine the strength of a business over time by
the amount of agony they go through in raising prices."*
WARREN BUFFET, chairman and CEO of Berkshire Hathaway

PRICING IS THE MOST impactful change you can make to your business. Not marketing. Not your website. Not even your employees. Those things are crucial, but adjusting your pricing is the number-one most significant change you can make. Period.

If you don't believe us, you should ask Dan McGuire—he's an incredible SaaS founder (and SaaS Academy coach) out of the U.K. with multiple exits –his most recent company, cube19, was acquired by Bullhorn in 2021.

When cube19 launched, Dan and his team saw some really solid growth—but after their first few years in business and their first few hundred customers, he had a realization:

> Despite the fact that we were already an expensive solution on the market, the reality was that we knew we were leaving money on the table. We were providing a ton of value, and our customers were

happy—but after those first few years, it was time to take a look at our pricing.

Dan ran the numbers and figured that on average, the price could probably come up by about 20 percent—but he didn't just drop a price increase on his customers and hope for the best. Instead, he gave them options:

- He built a list of his most important accounts that were already on long-term agreements so he knew which customers to exclude from the increase.

- He had 1:1 conversations with the other ones, told them about the price increase, and offered them a choice of preserving their existing price in exchange for upgrading to a three-year contract.

- He looked at their plans and added new modules, professional services, and enhanced customer support in order to sweeten the deal.

The emphasis on long term contracts and expansion-oriented pricing gave them incredibly durable revenue—their expansion revenue outpaced their churn (achieving the coveted Net-Negative Revenue Churn milestone), and their ARPA increased over 10 percent when it was all said and done.

But the best part? *They didn't lose a single customer from the price increase.* Because they'd done such a great job keeping their customers happy and delivering massive value over the years, the price increase was very well-received. Many of cube19's customers were thrilled to commit to multi-year contracts, and that stable revenue gave Dan the foundation he needed to successfully sell the company a few years later.

***

The biggest thing founders usually worry about when it comes to raising prices is losing customers. If you think that a 10 or 20 percent increase will cause a mass exodus, don't fret—as long as your customers like your product and you follow the process we're going to teach you in this chapter, you'll probably be fine. But again, don't take our word for it—*do the math instead:*

- If you increase your prices by 20 percent, you can afford to let go of 17 percent of your clients.

- Increase prices by 30 percent, you can afford to lose 23 percent of your clients.

- Even if you *double* your prices, you could afford to lose 50 percent of your customers and still break even.

Those churn numbers are generally "worst-case" scenarios—founders classically overestimate how many clients will leave and are pleasantly surprised when the biggest numerical change they see is in their revenue going up, not their customer count going down.

You're Playing the ARPA Game

When it comes to EXPANSION revenue, a.k.a. **Making Customers More Valuable**, you've got to know the game you're playing. And that game is one where you maximize the average revenue per account—which is what enables you to actually grow past your cost structures and re-invest in your business.

It's not about greed—it's about a fair trade of money for value. We talked about this in the last chapter; a world-class SaaS company is delivering ten times return-on-investment to their customers.

For most SaaS companies that we've worked with, delivering value isn't the problem—it's actually the *inverse*. Once founders find product-market fit, they're SO hesitant to change their pricing that they end up giving *too much away*—which hamstrings their growth, restricts their ability to hire team members and improve the product, and puts them on the fast track to mediocrity.

So, here's a big idea:

> **If you haven't raised your prices in the last year...you should raise them. Like, today.**

How do we know this? Simple—Patrick told us.

Patrick Campbell, who we mentioned before, is the founder of ProfitWell—and he's also a math god. He spent years working for a certain three-letter intelligence agency, literally using numbers to hunt down bad guys—and then, he went on to work at Google where he said he "used basically the same approach, but he was hunting for money instead." After those adventures, he switched gears to start ProfitWell, where he bootstrapped its growth and led the company through a $200 million acquisition by Paddle in 2022.

Long story short, Patrick knows his stuff. At one point in time, nearly one out of every five SaaS companies had their analytics plugged into ProfitWell's platform. Based on that data, Patrick found that most bootstrapped SaaS companies only update their pricing once every three years.

Once. Every. Three. Years.

Think back for a minute—where was your company three years ago? How did the product work? What was the team like? Did it even exist three years ago?

Over a three-year time horizon, we're pretty confident that almost every company has:

- Gained a better understanding of how to help their customers
- Shipped new features on their platform (likely without charging for it)
- Fixed a ton of bugs, increased speed and stability, and made other quality-of-life improvements.
- Built new integrations, updated databases, streamlined activation flows, and a ton of other improvements.

Yet...despite all of that added value...these same companies don't think they're worthy of increasing their prices.

Bill Wilson (who you heard from in the last chapter) says it like this: "The biggest mistake I see founders make around pricing is not changing it. If you haven't changed your price in years, it's effectively a price decrease."

If you think that sounds crazy...well, you're not wrong. But the resistance to changing pricing isn't rooted in logic—it's rooted in emotion. For some reason, founders get very emotional when it comes to changing their pricing—particularly for their existing customers. "What if everyone gets pissed? What if they leave? What if I burn the whole business down?" These are all very real fears that we've coached hundreds of founders through.

The unlock here is that you've got to make pricing decisions (and most other decisions) through an analytical lens instead of an emotional one. Frank Slootman, a legendary CEO (most recently of Snowflake) who has had three IPOs in his career, focuses quite a bit on decision-making in his book, Amp It Up. He says that to make great decisions, it "requires intellectual honesty—the ability to stay rational and set aside our biases and past experiences."

That's what we're going to do in this chapter—we're going to help you think unemotionally about raising your prices and give you a battle-tested framework to actually execute it.

And we'll start off with some cold, hard data. Patrick analyzed the numbers across 13,000 mid-market B2B SaaS companies, and here's what he found:

> ## The companies that revised their pricing once every quarter grew at least 4 times faster than those who did it once every 3 years.

What if your company could grow revenues four times faster than it does now? It'd be worth getting over this fear and fixing your pricing, right?

Of course it would. And that's why we're harping on this point. But we're not just going to convince you that you should raise your prices and send you on your way. We're about to walk through exactly how to increase prices without losing all your customers. In fact, if you run the play the way we write it in this chapter, you should lose very few.

But more importantly, even if you do lose a few customers, you'll still be in the black from a revenue standpoint. Dan's story from cube19 in the beginning of this chapter was a perfect example—sure, he lost a small a handful of customers, but his ARPA had a double-digit increase and his churn plummeted to almost nothing—he came out way ahead.

Losing a few customers isn't the worst thing in the world—as long as you're *actually playing the ARPA game,* and your revenue increases at the same time. You'll end up with more time and more money to invest in your best users, with fewer distractions and fewer support tickets.

Shrinking the Top of the Funnel

Let's say you're running your sales calls using the Rocket Demo Builder™ framework like we taught you in chapter 5, and you're closing 40 percent of your deals. If your current deal size is $2,500 annually and your goal is to add $100,000 in ARR, you'll need to conduct 100 sales calls in order to hit your goal. With a show rate of 50 percent, you'll need to schedule 200 calls on your calendar.

200 calls scheduled * 50% show rate = 100 calls conducted
100 calls conducted * 40% win rate = 40 new customers
40 new customers * $2,500 ACV (annual contract value) = $100,000 in ARR

That's all good and well. It's doable. But you know we're going to ask: what if you raised your prices?

Let's say you increase your ACV by 20 percent—from $2,500 to $3,000. If every other number remains the same, you're looking at *thirty less calls scheduled* in order to generate the same $100,000 in revenue. Even if your close rate decreases a bit, you'll still generate more revenue than before...but that's not even the best part.

Since you need less calls scheduled, your CAC will likely decrease as well. You'll need fewer leads to create the calls, less calendar time to generate the revenue, and less deals to pay commission on. Even if revenue broke even, you're still running a more efficient (read: profitable) operation at the new price point.

If you're still not convinced, you can head over to softwarebook.com/pricing and use our calculator to see the impact of a pricing change on your funnel. We've done the hard work for you—you just need to plug in your numbers.

***

Alright—so you've seen the math. But you might still feel uneasy about increasing your prices. It's cool—that's totally normal.

It's also why we've included Patrick's exact email template that you can use to tell your customers about what's coming. But before we get too excited and start firing off emails...there's a bit of pre-work that we need to knock out.

Not All Customers Are Created Equal

First things first—if you haven't read the previous chapter on how to create a world-class pricing structure, go back and read it. The Pricing Triangle is a super succinct explanation of some of the most potent pricing drivers in SaaS—and running the playbook in this chapter without building a solid structure in the first place is just going to be wasted effort.

Shoring up your pricing structure will give you the confidence you need to run this play—not only because you'll be confident in the outcome, but you'll also be confident in the reasoning behind the pricing changes in the first place.

Your price is not just your cost with a markup. Our friend Lincoln Murphy, who runs Sixteen Ventures and is the author of the legendary book *Customer Success*, says very clearly that "pricing should be an input—NOT a result on a spreadsheet." Or, like Patrick says, "we're not trading wheat for goats anymore." Instead of "covering your cost," you should be putting a dollar estimate on the value you're creating for your customers and working backwards from that.

Alright—so we're on the same page that we should be anchoring our price around the value we provide, which means that there's likely some opportunity to raise prices for your existing customers. Dan's assessment (after personally coaching thousands of founders):

> **On average, most companies can raise their prices 20% with minimal downside.**

And that's an average, not a limit. We've met founders who could straight away double, triple, or even ten times their prices (no joke). But regardless of whether it's a 5 percent increase or a 100 percent increase, you'll need to manage it the same way.

Stack Rank the Impact

Most businesses do their first major price increase to "bring customers up to market value." What this means is that there are likely a variety of customers at a variety of old price points, and your goal is to bring them all up to the current price.

And the key to pulling this off without losing a whole bunch of customers? You've got to tailor the communication strategy based on how much the customer is impacted. We'll explain.

First, enter your entire customer list into a spreadsheet (you can snag a template for this at softwarebook.com/increase). The spreadsheet should list out the customer identifier (like email address or customer number), their current price point, their new price point, and the percentage change between the two. Lastly, sort descending by the percentage change.

You've now created an impact assessment—in other words, a stack-ranked list of your customers with the biggest impact at the top.

> **A customer who is receiving a 50% increase requires a different approach than a customer who is receiving a 5% increase.**

There are typically three levels of outreach that we see most companies take:

1. **1:1 Founder / CEO Outreach:** All of your VIP accounts as well as customers that are high ACV and experiencing a major price increase

2.   **1:1 CS Team Outreach:** All of your average ACV accounts that are experiencing a major price increase

3.   **Email Outreach:** Any accounts not falling into the first two categories (which will typically be the majority of your accounts)

What constitutes a "major" price increase? That's up to you—it depends on a lot of factors, such as annual contract value, dollar value of the increase, customer concentration risk[15], and more. It's ok to follow your gut on this one...to a point. Just don't use it as an excuse not to run the price increase.

Regardless of category, the "talk track" is the same. Here's the exact message you can use (written as an email):

The Ultimate Price-Increase Method™

This is a three-part email template that's hand-crafted to gently inform your customers about price increases. Anything you see in <brackets> is a field that should be customized to either the recipient or the company.

Please make sure you get the customization right (especially if you're tempted to copy/paste from a digital version of this book). Emailing someone about a price increase and literally calling them <First Name> doesn't go over too well.

One last thing—you'll notice that the language is straightforward, and even casual at times. This is by design. When legendary founder Eoghan McCabe (CEO of Intercom) was asked in an AMA[16] about the "one most important part of customer communication," this was his answer:

---

[15] Customer Concentration Risk: A situation where a large percentage of your revenue is generated by a small percentage of your accounts. In this case, those key accounts should be handled with care – personally.

[16] AMA stands for "Ask Me Anything" – it's essentially a Q&A session where the participant fields whatever questions come their way.

"It's critical to be real, be personal, and be human. Think of every shit communication you've experienced recently—untargeted, spammy, fake emails. It's the opposite of personal."

This email template follows that advice to the letter. It's personalized, genuine, written in a way that honors the relationship, and is sent by a real human being. If you want it to work well, please don't stray from these principles—because it's written this way for a reason.

Ok, here goes:

<First Name>,

Over the past <12> months, we've added so much value to <Company>:

- We've made you <$18,418>
- Feature A <is now standard in your account>
- Feature B <is awesome, and you use it daily>

For us to continue to invest in making <Company> better for you and the <Customer Company> crew, we need to increase our prices.

You've been insanely loyal to <Company> though—using us for the last <four and a half> years. As of today, we're raising prices for *new* customers, but since you've been so loyal we're going to keep you on your existing plan for the next 6 months (after which we'll bump you up to the new price of <$X, XXX>.

Thanks for being an integral part of the <Company> mission. If you have any questions at all, please let me know—all replies go directly to me.

<CEO Name>

> P.S. If this materially impacts your business, let me know and we'll
> work something out.

That's the email (and you can grab an editable copy at
softwarebook.com/increase)—now, let's break it down to understand
why it works.

Step 1: Quantify the Value You've Provided

In any pricing-related conversation, the first thing you want to do is
provide some data around the value you've provided for your customer.
In a perfect world, this won't be the first time they've seen this
information—it should also be on their dashboard when they log in,
contained in summary emails that get sent out, etc.

But if not...even if you need to manually calculate or estimate it...now is
the time to do it.

Here's an example of how this first section works. The email is coming
from a company called Copyscape, that uses AI to create podcast show
notes and blog posts—and we're sending it to a customer named Julie
who runs a business of her own called PodcastOwl.

> Hey Julie!
>
> We're stoked you've been a part of our growth these last thirteen
> months. Since then, we've refined and upgraded our AI model,
> which has helped you produce 100 show notes and over 200 blog
> posts from your podcast recordings and videos. It's saved you at least
> 650 hours and $16,250 in content creation.

For us to continue to invest in making Copyscape better for you and your team at PodcastOwl, we need to increase our prices.

In the example above, we're quickly pointing out the number of hours and money saved thanks to the product. It's also the right time to highlight major feature additions or upgrades. It's important to remind the customer that you're dedicated to improving their experience with your software—and that you're not just trying to grab their cash.

And then the important part: **Tell them in plain English that this is a price increase email.** There's nothing worse than companies that try to "hide" the price increase information at the bottom of a long email. After using the Pricing Triangle to craft your new pricing strategy, you should be confident in your message (even if you're also a bit nervous). Don't act like you've got something to hide.

Also, while we're on the topic of things not to do: NEVER use inflation as a reason to raise prices. A few months ago, a member of our team got a message like this from their behemoth corporate landlord about some office space. They were telling the truth—inflation *had* forced them to raise prices. But if it's affecting you, it's also affecting your customers—and this is more likely to make them angry with you than to get you the sympathy you're shooting for. Apologizing for raising prices is a bad look—instead, you should be able to legitimately justify the increase based on the value you're creating.

Or to say it differently, don't try to get away with raising your prices just because the cost of milk has gone up.

Step 2: Reward Their Loyalty

You've got to thank the customer for being part of your company's growth—however long they've been with you. You might feel like this part isn't that important or that you can skip it—but you're wrong.

> ## People don't remember what you said, they remember how you made them feel.

This is why it's so important. It's not a "magic sentence," but it lets the customer know that they're more than just a revenue line item—that you actually know how long they've been with you and that you're taking the time to recognize it.

But of course, talk is cheap—and just saying thanks isn't going to be enough. We've got to actually give them something in exchange for their loyalty. And in this case, we're going to give them an additional six months of breathing room before their price increase kicks in.

The goal here is to lower the barrier to continuing on with your company in the short term. Customers are most likely to churn from a price increase immediately after it happens, so by pushing the effective date out six months, you're significantly defusing that risk. Plus, it makes them feel like a VIP, which is never a bad thing.

NOTE: What you don't want to do is grandfather them in forever. Grandfathering customers forever can be a kiss of death for your ARPA (and your company)—and it also digs a hole that's much tougher to dig out of later. If you wonder how companies end up having to raise prices by 50 percent or more for some of their customers, it's usually correcting for grandfathered prices that were way too low for way too long.

The language we use is simple (continuing our example):

You've been insanely loyal to Copyscape—you've used us for the last thirteen months! So as of today, we're raising prices for new customers, but since you've been so loyal we're going to keep you on your existing plan for the next 6 months (after which we'll bump you up to the new price of $249 per month).

That's all it takes. They'll feel special, you'll be much less likely to lose a customer, and you did it all without permanently grandfathering people in for old price points.

There's just one more part to this whole thing—it's the one that makes people the most nervous and is also the one that you definitely can't skip.

Step 3: Leave Them a Safety Net

People generally hate being told what to do—especially if you're selling to other entrepreneurs. So, if for whatever reason they get super enraged about the price increase or it causes them a major cash flow headache, we want to give them an additional option—to have a 1:1 conversation with you about their situation.

It's all in how you close the email:

Thanks for being an integral part of the Copyscape mission. If you have any questions at all, please let me know—all replies go directly to me.

- James

P.S. If this materially impacts your business, let me know and we'll work something out.

Simply seeing that you're treating them like human beings and that you're willing to have a conversation goes an incredibly long way. And if that last line makes you nervous, you're not alone—when Patrick taught this framework from the SaaS Academy stage, many founders had the same question. Good news is that Patrick is a data guy—and he's run this play across thousands of companies with one consistent result:

The replies they got were overwhelmingly positive, especially when the increase was reasonable (NPS scores predictably take a massive hit when price increases are over 50 percent, for instance).

And when you do get a reply? It's all good—train your team to have some sort of salvage offer that helps them bridge an additional three to six months if needed—without offering a permanent discount. It's still better for your company to have a few customers that you saved with a salvage offer vs. losing them outright.

***

By sending this email, you've created a flow of information that makes it clear what's happening. You've justified a price increase with customized data about the results you've driven for your customers. You were upfront with them that the price needs to change in order to keep improving the product. You've honored their loyalty and eliminated short-term impact with a six-month buffer. And if all that's not enough, you gave them the opportunity to talk it out with you.

Most people aren't going to read your message and get upset. They'll get it. Knowing your break-even numbers and cross-referencing it against the impact spreadsheet you created earlier will help you flag potential concerns—which lets you have a plan for handling those customers ahead of time. If there's a customer that's been with you for two years that's about to get a 45 percent price increase...I'd expect them to call you. And when you do, you'll have a plan of action ready to go.

The price point of your software and how much margin you have on your break-even numbers will drive how flexible you can be with your salvage offers. If you get a concerned reply from a loyal customer, you have space to negotiate—but if a customer that wasn't really a fit anyway blasts you for a 4 percent increase, you'll know that you can afford to stand strong.

Work to accommodate your most loyal, best-fit customers—and the rest of the cards will fall where they fall.

Locking In Long-Term Pricing

When you're executing a price increase, it's also a perfect time to lock in some long-term pricing deals. With a lot of the same messaging that you've already learned, you can give customers the option to lock in your current pricing for a full year...as long as they pay in advance.

You already heard one example of Dan McGuire running this play at the beginning of this chapter—but if you want another example, check out how Russ Perry, founder and CEO of Design Pickle and SaaS Academy alum, approached it:

Design Pickle's Annual Pricing

Hi Matt,

I wanted to send a friendly reminder that we will be archiving our original plans based on our old pricing of $370/mo.

But never fear — you can get "grandfathered" into our lower rates until we officially archive the older plans on <u>July 1st.</u>

So here are your options:

1. Sign up for a **quarterly plan** for $1119 and get locked into the OG $370/mo pricing.
2. Sign up for **semi-annual plan** for $1999 and get locked into the OG $370/mo AND enjoy a 10% discount for as long as you remain a client.
3. Sign up for an **annual plan** for $3552 and get locked into the OG $370/mo pricing AND enjoy a 20% discount for as long as you remain a client.

Think about it—traditional SaaS strategy says to offer an annual plan at a discount of ten-to-twenty percent...but this is a chance to bypass that discount entirely by offering it at your full price—before the increase[17]. Especially if you're self-funded, it's also a great way to pull cash forward for reinvestment in the business.

Subscription Management Tooling

If you've made it this far in this chapter, you're probably ready to go raise your prices. But there's one tricky part to this whole thing that is an

---

[17] In this example, Russ chose to stack the current pricing AND a discount – but that's not a *required* part of running this strategy.

incredible "momentum killer" for SaaS companies trying to run this play: the technical lift of actually changing the prices in your software.

Here's how it tends to go:

Non-Technical Founder: "Hey, CTO! What's up? It's time to change our pricing. Should be pretty easy, right?

CTO: "Umm...I'm not sure. Pricing touches a lot of stuff in the platform. We'll probably have to slot it into a sprint or two next quarter.

Non-Technical Founder: "Why can't we just do it this week?"

*CTO: *rage**

This is incredibly common—especially if it's your first price increase, or if you're introducing variable components like depth-of-usage or feature fencing for the first time. Most companies in the past decade or so started the same way—build a Stripe integration, tie the plans directly into their codebase, set it, and forget it.

If you're bumping into this in your company, it's probably time for a subscription management tool of some sort. Remember back to the beginning of this chapter—Patrick taught us that companies that adjust their pricing on a quarterly basis grow four times faster than the "once every three years" group.

> ## We're not advocating that you change pricing for your existing customers quarterly.

But running higher-frequency tests on new sales in order to validate whether or not the price point is a good idea? You should be able to do that whenever you want—and a subscription management platform is what keeps you out of the engineering backlog and into your pricing experiments.

So, our recommendation is that if you're staring at significant rework to deploy your first pricing change...instead of doing that, use the roadmap time to implement a subscription management tool. The juice is worth the squeeze—because 4x faster growth is 4x faster growth. You can thank us later.

***

Hopefully, you now understand the main reasons why SaaS businesses don't change their prices:

1. They aren't aware how drastically it can impact your bottom line
2. They don't have the language to deploy the price increase
3. They have a fear about the majority of their customer base churning
4. They have technical limitations that make it difficult to test new price points

We've addressed all of those issues in this chapter—leaving no excuse not to adjust your prices whenever you deem it necessary. You have every tool you need right here in this book.

But there's one more element to **Making Clients More Valuable** that we haven't touched on yet—and it's one that Marcel is particularly passionate about. We might even go to war with some generally accepted venture capitalist lore in the process.

5 Hot Principles

1. **Pricing is a process, not an event:** Companies that regularly experiment with pricing grow four times faster than companies that don't. Nailing pricing models that capture more value and encourage EXPANSION and RETENTION is the wisest play you implement to improve your SaaS business.

2. **Don't be scared:** Most founders are afraid of raising their prices. Our data on thousands of price increases shows that when it's

done right, the risk versus reward analysis makes this a total no-brainer.

3. **Stack rank the impact:** Don't go into a price increase with blinders on. Make a list of your customers and calculate how pricing changes will impact them so you can tailor your communication to their situation.

4. **Use The Ultimate Price-Increase Method™:** Don't reinvent the wheel—just use the template! Remember to remind your customers of the value you've delivered, justify the increase, reward them for their loyalty, and have salvage offers ready for anyone who is seriously impacted. Oh, and never (ever) grandfather your customers indefinitely.

5. **Fix your tech stack:** Don't let your technical debt stop you from fixing your pricing. You may have to do some work but install a subscription management platform so you only have to do it once—and then you can be incredibly agile deploying pricing changes in the future.

The Next Right Move

Armed with these templates, it's time for you to execute your first pricing increase. It doesn't have to be complicated. Just taking the pricing you have today and increase it by 10 to 20 percent if you want to keep it simple.

In Dan's famous words, it's time to JFDI (just f*cking do it). Lock in your commitment to increase your price by a specific date:

I'll increase my pricing by _____ % on _____, 20_____.

Now—make your spreadsheet, grab the pricing increase email template at softwarebook.com/increase, and get to work.

CHAPTER 11

You're Already a Services Company (Here's How to Charge for It)

"If ARR could be maximized without a professional services team or function, then no company would have one."[xvi]
DAVE KELLOGG, executive in residence at Balderton Capital

BACK IN CHAPTER 6, you met Brad Redding, CEO of Elevar. Like most SaaS founders, Brad and his team were maniacally focused on one thing—increasing MRR. And they knew that by getting their customers to First Value quickly and consistently, those customers would stick around much longer, spend more money over time, and be more likely to recommend their product to others.

There was just one problem: Because they had a technical product designed to solve a complex problem, Brad and his team were investing a ton into onboarding. Plus, most of their clients needed customization, meaning Elevar had to have very skilled experts on hand during the onboarding process.

Elevar's sky-high onboarding expenses were delaying their CAC Payback Period. Yet, regardless of how intensive the onboarding process was, Brad knew it was still necessary: customers who didn't get to First Value quickly were likely to churn, pulling Elevar's Growth Ceiling forward and putting the business at risk. From that standpoint, they couldn't afford not to invest time and money into onboarding. Brad was stuck.

VCs Are Wrong About Services

Venture capitalists love the SaaS business model, and they typically turn their noses up at services companies. In fact, you've probably heard that adding services will actually decrease the value of your SaaS company, even if your revenue increases because of those services. And yes, if two-thirds of your revenue comes from you suddenly transforming from a SaaS company into a marketing agency, your valuation may decrease. However, if you build your services the right way (which we're going to show you in this chapter), those services will actually make your SaaS company more valuable over time.

SaaS businesses require a lot of human effort to build, scale, and support the company. Consider how many of these jobs you're already doing today:

- Onboarding and configuration
- Customer support (email, phone, live chat, 1:1 sessions, etc.)
- Quarterly business reviews with large clients
- Custom implementation services
- Customer-requested feature development
- Custom integrations

Not only do these roles sustain your business, they directly drive MRR. And therein lies the dirty little secret about SaaS companies:

> ## The main difference between a *SaaS* company and a *services* company is that SaaS companies tend to give away their services for free.

Don't believe us? Go back to the list we just showed you and think about how many of those jobs you're currently doing (and how many of those you aren't charging for). You justify providing these services (usually for free) because you know if you don't provide them, your customers won't have success with your product, which means they'd churn.

But here's a reality check: If you're providing 1:1 implementation and setup, priority support, or custom integrations, someone's paying for that. And right now, that someone is probably you. Which is exactly what got Brad at Elevar pondering a great question:

> ## "What if, instead of doing this stuff for free, we charged money for some of it?"

At first, most of Brad's team fought the idea. Like most of us, they'd drank the standard VC Kool-Aid: *"Services are bad in a SaaS company."* But eventually, Brad's team "got it": In order to keep their world-class customer service, they'd need to turn those services cost centers into revenue-generating activities. In turn, they could bring money forward and then invest that money into improving customer success, driving up activation and retention all along the way.

So, Brad's team went from offering complementary concierge onboarding to charging $500 for the same service.

They were all expecting a drop in sales.

But fast-forward a few weeks, and the team was shocked—no one flinched. Their win rate stayed exactly the same, except now, they had an extra $500 in cash from every new sale that they could pull forward to keep creating one of the world's premier SaaS products. Oh, and as a bonus, customers in their onboarding program suddenly become more engaged: as soon as Brad and his team repositioned onboarding as a paid service, customers started taking the process more seriously. It's like Dan always says:

"People who pay, pay attention."

We don't want you to get lost in services. The goal has been (and always will be) to build a world-class SaaS company. Period. But to do that, you're going to need equally world-class support, onboarding, integrations, and whatever else your customers need to win. And you don't need to provide all that for free.

The Two Services Every SaaS Company Probably Already Has. . . But Should Charge For

The most important takeaway from this story is that Brad and his team didn't "invent" some professional service to offer in order to make money. They simply monetized the services that they were already providing. This allowed them to remove financial constraints in their onboarding process, leading to improved customer success, higher retention, and better cash flow.

While you could technically charge for any of the services you're already providing, we've found through experience that there are two services almost every SaaS company should be charging for:

1: Customer Onboarding

The first is paid onboarding, also known as "implementation." You just saw this at work in Brad's story above. Essentially, these are setup fees. When customers receive one-on-one help to get started, they're more likely to activate—which makes them more likely to stick around for the long haul. That leaves one looming question: how much should you be charging for this service? Here's the short answer:

> **Most SaaS companies can sell paid implementation for between 10% and 20% of their annual contract value. . . *without* impacting sales.**

We've run this specific play with over a hundred companies inside of SaaS Academy, and the founders are always blown away. In many cases, not only are they making sales at the same rate as before, but their customers are happy to pay the money for the service, because by receiving implementation, they're more likely to get the result they wanted in the first place.

There's another hidden benefit to launching paid onboarding that most people don't consider: It gives you something to give away. In our eyes, discounting your MRR should be a last resort, yet, many teams reach for it as a tool to pull deals forward and create urgency. So, once you have paid onboarding as part of your offer stack, you can discount or give away the service, which again, is something you were probably doing anyway. That allows you to keep your MRR at full price.

> **If you've got to sacrifice some revenue to get a deal done, sacrifice the services revenue and protect the MRR.**

2: Priority Support

At a recent SaaS Academy event, we invited Patrick Campbell from ProfitWell (whom you learned about in the last chapter) to talk about pricing strategies. He revealed that there was one add-on service that was underutilized across the entire SaaS industry and the companies that implemented it were crushing: priority support. Here's why this works:

> ## Most people will pay a little extra to skip to the front of the line.

Disney has proven this with their Genie+ offerings (formerly FastPass+). It's a premium pass that a visitor can purchase to skip the line on popular rides. These cost between $15 and $30 each (on an average admission price of $160) and are estimated to generate over $300 million in revenue for Disney. Go back and run those numbers—it's roughly between 10 and 20 percent of the "deal size" (a.k.a. the cost of admission).[18]

And guess what? That datapoint holds true for offering priority support to other businesses, too. Patrick analyzed data across thousands of SaaS companies who started charging for priority support, and he found that "almost invariably, about 20 percent of your customers will willingly opt-in to pay for priority support."[19]

> ## Patrick's rule of thumb is to start at 10% of your ACV[20] for a priority support offering.

So, if you're selling a $1,000 per-year deal, offer priority support as a $100 add-on. If 20 percent of your existing customers opted-in for an add-on service that generated a 10 percent lift in their annual revenue for charging for something you already provide, wouldn't that be a good outcome?

The great thing about offering priority support is that it's *risk free*. It's completely optional, can be offered to the customers you already have,

---

[18] As of July 2024, Disney just released an even newer offering called Lightning Lane Multi Pass.
[19] Said live at a SaaS Academy event.
[20] If you need a quick reminder, ACV stands for Annual Contract Value – the amount your charge a customer over the course of one year.

and it doesn't change anything if they don't want it. There's very little downside.

The SaaS Services Planner™

We recommend you start simply with one of the two services above. But if you already have those in place or they aren't a great fit for you, the rest of this chapter will show you exactly how to build a professional services offering that supports your customers, your MRR, *and* your bottom line.

Before we get into it, we need to remind you about one key principle:

> ### Customers will stick around as long as your company is solving their problems.

Notice we didn't just say as long as your *product* is solving their problems.

Many times, your product isn't the issue, or at least not the only one. Your customers might have to jump through hurdles *before* they can get any value from your SaaS platform, and some of those hurdles might be issues your software doesn't solve. These customer hurdles could be technical issues such as account provisioning and data migration, all the way up to high-level challenges such as organizational behavior change or overcoming limiting beliefs, all of which can get in the way of your customer's own success.

The trickiest part of this whole thing is your mindset: You're a software founder, so you're naturally going to look for problems that can be solved with software solutions. But if all you have is a hammer, everything looks like a nail. . . and that's exactly where Marcel and his co-founder Ben found themselves in the early days of Parakeeto.

The two co-founders had been building Parakeeto for almost three years, and like many of the companies we've featured in this book, they were jammed up. They'd had some early wins and truly believed in the business, but they hadn't yet found product-market fit. They were stuck firmly at $10,000 in MRR for almost a year (an early Growth Ceiling).

It was a painful situation—they'd built their company to help digital agencies fix their profitability, and they knew that it was a real problem. Still, they couldn't get their customers to use their software to fix it.

The pressure was mounting, so Ben and Marcel made an agreement: If they didn't start seeing traction in the upcoming quarter, they'd call it quits. They set specific goals around what "traction" would look like, and even negotiated the terms of their breakup if it came to that.

Fast forward three months...and they were in the same spot. No revenue growth. But instead of calling it quits like they'd agreed, the two co-founders felt an unignorable desire to stay the course. They'd spent so much time on calls with customers learning about their pain points that they were both more convinced that they could solve the problem—even if the numbers weren't there yet. As Marcel put it, "We knew there was oil. We just weren't drilling in the right place yet". So, they gave it another three months, following a cycle nearly every SaaS founder is familiar with:

- Get customer feedback and analyze product analytics
- Determine which problem to solve next
- Brainstorm solution to the problem
- Design the features and write the specs
- Build the features
- Test the user experience
- Tweak, tune, and fix the bugs
- Write the press release
- Ship the new features
- Hope for a million users

And after that? Yep, you guessed it—still nothing. So they went another quarter. And another. They were learning, talking to customers, building software, and doing everything else they could think of—but the Growth Ceiling was holding strong, and they couldn't seem to break through.

After four quarters of this infuriating cycle, Marcel finally asked Ben the one question that would change everything:

"What if we weren't confined to just software? What if we didn't have to worry about scalability, or even about profitability? What would we build in order to solve our customers' problems better than anyone else in the world?"

The answer to that question not only saved their company, but it built the framework that we're about to teach you in this chapter. Because, as we mentioned earlier, there is a right way for a SaaS company to offer professional services. In about ten minutes, you'll be armed with everything you need in order to pull that off—without tanking your valuation or your profit margins.

The tool is called the SaaS Services Planner™, and it outlines the three key steps to nailing any professional services offer:

The SaaS Services Planner

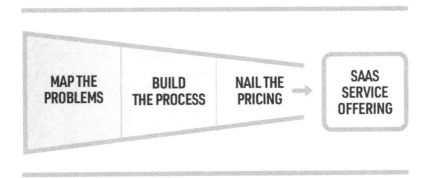

Seem simple? It is. But, like most things, the devil is in the details, and without following all three steps, you'll run the risk of not solving the right problem for your customers, or doing it at a price point that isn't viable for the long term.

Phase 1: Map the Problems

Remember Marcel's question from earlier? When he asked what they'd need to build if they stopped worrying about being a software company?

That's exactly where you need to start, too.

Your end goal is to build a world-class SaaS company, not a services company. But doing that will likely require you to solve other problems that are standing in the way. . . and those problems are often solved with non-software solutions. Think about it like this—if you build a gym, but you don't have a parking lot or lockers, customers won't be able to use your gym. Now, you don't want to become a parking-lot builder or a locker company, but you need to have those items available so that your gym can grow.

Back to Marcel and Ben: They started by writing down all the problems their customers were facing. And next to each problem, they wrote down a way that they could solve it, regardless of whether or not it involved their software.

When they started thinking about their company as a holistic solution, and decoupled it from software, they were able to create a product that their customers loved (and their revenue growth proved it—more on that later).

Here's the takeaway:

> ## As a founder, it's your job to know everything that stands between your customers and their goals.

And in order to do that, you need to do three things:

1. Clearly identify your customer's *starting point* as well as their *ideal end state*.

2. Document *every action* that needs to happen in order to get from where they are now to that end state (whether those actions include your platform or not).

3. Identify every problem and challenge that the customer will face during each step (these are the opportunities).[21]

Usually, these three elements are visualized using sticky notes on a wall (if you're old-school) or a whiteboard-style software tool (if you're fancy). Either way, you want to make things easy for you and the collaborators on your team to understand.

> ## Your job is to map *every step* of the journey, not just the ones that have to do with your software.

For instance, let's say a new user has to upload a spreadsheet of their clients into your billing platform. This task seems simple, but can actually be pretty complicated for your customer—they likely need to export the data, download an import template, format the data a certain way, remove duplicates, etc. Those annoying details create the friction

---

[21] Most people call this exercise Customer Journey Mapping – we've got a free template for you at softwarebook.com/services.

that often pushes your customers to bail. But these issues shouldn't frustrate *you*. . . because they show you where the opportunities lie.

If you've followed our advice, you'll end up staring at a wall full of sticky notes. At that point, your job becomes simple: Find the most interesting opportunities and come up with solutions.

Here's a quick start guide to point you in the right direction:

1. You should have a step-by-step map of your customers' journey. As you follow the path, make a list of every single problem that frustrate your customers that your software doesn't solve today.

2. Rank those problems in priority order—not by how much you think you could charge, but by the risk those hurdles pose to your software MRR. In other words, focus on the problems that are most likely to cause software churn if left unsolved.

3. Look for patterns. For instance, are three of the top five problems in your ranked list all things that happen during the activation period?

The end result? You'll have a list of problems that you can solve for your customers, all of which will serve them and help you retain your most valuable asset—MRR.

Now, pick (at least) one!

Phase 2: Build the Process

So, we've identified (at least) one customer problem you can solve that drives MRR.

Now, take your customer's current process for solving the problem and make it better, make it faster, or simply do it for them.

Don't overthink this part. Keep it simple. Pick the biggest problem your customer has that puts your MRR at risk. Figure out a process to solve it. Test it with a customer. Repeat it a few times. Make it better. Keep going.

We can't stress this too much: Don't turn this into a second business. Don't hire a half dozen people. Don't go read fifteen blog posts on time-tracking and job-costing and agency operations and scaling creative teams and call centers and whatever else is out there. You don't need to build an in-house agency. You need to simply solve the problem. Remember, we're doing this to help your customer have an amazing experience so they stick around—which drives improved retention and higher MRR. Plus, you're probably already providing services that solve some of the problems you identified, so you might as well charge for them and make your customers more valuable, too.

Now, let's get to the exciting part—building the offer.

Phase 3: Nail the Pricing

Just like your SaaS platform, getting your services pricing right is a huge lever. Without it, you can do a ton of work and solve all the world's problems and still end up without the cash you need to keep running your business.

There are three steps to pricing services, but it all starts with one key decision—your margin target.

A: Set Your Margin Target

When we ask most founders about how much margin they want to make on services, they usually say one of two things:

1. "Nothing really, just enough to cover my costs."
2. "As much as humanly possible."

Like most things, the right answer lies somewhere in the middle. The primary reason you're offering these services is to support and retain your software customers—and the secondary reason is to make money. But we also want to keep you rooted in reality: everything is more expensive than you think it is, and for that reason, if you plan to break even or make a profit, we recommend targeting at least a 40 percent margin.

Here are some general guidelines for setting a margin target:

- Up to 40%: Allows you to recover at least some of the cost.
- 50%: Allows you to consistently break even.
- 60%: Typically enables you to make a modest profit.
- 70% and up: Usually creates enough cash to fund growth.

If these percentages feel high to you, there's a reason: unutilized time eats up 10 to 20 percent of your margin (internal meetings, time off, holidays, etc.). Overhead costs typically take up another 20 to 30 percent, so overall, a 50 percent margin is right where you'll reliably break even. As an example, if you're charging $100 per month for premium support, in order to consistently break even, you'd need to plan on doing the work for $50 per month or less.

B: Estimate Your Delivery Costs

In order to price a service, you'll need to have an idea who will be doing the work (and how much they make) and how long the work will take (on an hourly basis).

For hourly team members, this is easy, but it can be a little tricker for full-time, salaried employees. To figure out their hourly cost, take their fully loaded salary (including benefits and taxes) and divide it by 2,080 (the typical amount of working hours in a year). Don't worry about time off, holidays, etc.; we factored all that into our margin target already.[22]

For example, if you have a team member that makes $100,000 in salary plus roughly $12,000 in benefit costs and taxes, you'd take $112,000 and divide it by 2,080 to get an effective hourly rate of $53.85.[23]

C: Calculate Your Perfect Price

There are two general pricing models when it comes to charging for services: hourly pricing and flat-fee pricing. As a general rule, we prefer flat-fee pricing because it's easier to sell and leaves more room to capture margin. But there's a downside: If you're not able to estimate how long the service will take to deliver, you can eat through your margin and have no way to recover. So, Marcel's got a killer rule for this:

> ## If you can estimate the delivery cost within 20%, use flat-fee pricing.

Here's the good news—when calculating your perfect price, it doesn't matter if you're using flat-fee pricing or hourly pricing. Either way, the final step is the same—you're going to divide your delivery cost by the number one minus your margin target (So, if your delivery cost is $60 an hour, and your margin target is 70 percent, then the math looks like this: $60 ÷ (1—.7) which means you should be charging $200 an hour.)

---

[22] Variables like this are why we set our "break even" margin target at 50 percent. It's easier to build a buffer than to plan for every nickel and dime we spend!

[23] The hourly rate gets a little more complicated if you're using multiple team members to deliver the service – you'll have to either count them separately, or just take an average salary and run the numbers with that. Again, you don't have to overthink this as long as you've followed our guidance on margins because you've got a healthy buffer to work with.

Full Example of Setting Price:

Let's run through an example of setting a price. Let's assume you own a SaaS company that

provides a data migration service.

Set Your Margin Target: In this case, your goal is just to recover some of the costs, because you know that data migration is a major unlock for product activation. So, you set your margin target at 40 percent.

Estimate Your Delivery Costs: For this service, you'll have a customer support rep doing the work. This team member makes $75,000 per year with a benefits cost of about $9,000 per year—which makes their total compensation about $84,000 per year. To get their hourly cost, you divide $84,000 by 2,080, which is $40.38 per hour. Lastly, you think this work will take about six hours to complete, which gives you a total delivery cost of $242.28 (let's call it $250 for easy math). You also assume that that estimate—six hours—will always be within 20 percent of actual costs, so, using Marcel's rule, you decide to use flat-fee pricing.

Calculate Your Perfect Price: To do this, divide your costs by 1—margin target: At this point, it's some simple math to find your price point:

$$\$250 / (1 - 0.4)$$
$$\$250 / 0.6$$
Price: $416.66

If you decided to charge hourly instead of fixed, just do the same math on the hourly rate (in this case, it would be $40.38 / (1—0.4), which would give you an hourly rate of about $67.

Regardless of which pricing model you choose, the math is simple—and charging a customer a few hundred bucks to save them the headache of migrating their own data is probably an easy conversation.

The moral of the story: Your customers need your help. You probably know all of the problems that they have that your product doesn't solve. And now you know how to solve them without doing it for free.

P.S.—(We imagine you can guess what we're going to say here!) If you want a quick calculator to help you run this math, head over to softwarebook.com/services.

A Note on High-Ticket Services

Ok, so $400 is one thing, but let's say you're performing a much higher-priced professional service, something to the tune of $18,000. It might feel harder to sell up front at that price point—and it probably will be—but the gold is in the terms. There are a lot of different ways that $18,000 can be expressed to a client:

1. It's $18,000
2. It's $6,000 per month for 3 months
3. It's $10,000 in data fees and $6,000 in consulting fees
4. It's 100 hours at $180 per hour
5. Etc.

No matter how we sliced it, the underlying margin didn't change. You can get creative with pricing structures, terms, and timing in order to make it fit the deal.

Pulling All Three Levers at Once

The wild thing about a well-designed services strategy is that it's one of the few tools that actually attacks all three levers simultaneously:

Lever 1: ACQUISITION—You're getting more customers by offering something that truly solves their problem (instead of just creating more work for them). You're also creating an offering that you can readily discount if that's what it takes to move the deal forward.

Lever II: RETENTION—You're retaining customers longer by annihilating every roadblock that stands behind them and their First Value moment. And, in some cases, you're even working with them in an ongoing fashion to guide them to success.

Lever III: EXPANSION—And of course, you're making customers more valuable by charging for the additional services you're providing at a healthy margin.

Marcel's story ended up almost exactly like this—when he and Ben followed what they now call the SaaS Services Planner™, they ended up creating three service offerings to supplement their SaaS platform. They found that customers needed to do a ton of work to get their time-tracking data organized (which was a blocker for getting value from the software), so, they helped them fix it. They also realized that migrating the data was painful, so, they offered that, too. Last but not least, they created a coaching and data-monitoring service to ensure their software's configuration and data structure evolved alongside their customers' businesses.

And when we said earlier that their customers loved it, we weren't kidding: Marcel and Ben added more MRR in one week after their new offer went live than they had in the prior eighteen months. From there, it was off to the races. Today, their revenue level is now in the multiple seven-figure range. All they had to do was look for their customers' biggest problems and provide a solution . . . even if that solution wasn't technically "software."

We said this in the introduction to this book, and it's incredibly fitting to say it again at the end of this final chapter:

> **Your competitive advantage isn't how you write your code. It's how you serve your customers.**

And Marcel's story proves it.

5 Hot Principles

1. **You're already a services company**: Whether you realize it or not, you're already providing a variety of "professional services" to your customers.

2. **Monetize your existing services:** You don't need to invent new things to do in order to subsidize your MRR with services revenue. Chances are, you're already providing services that you should be monetizing and building official infrastructure around.

3. **Onboarding and priority support:** Two of the quickest wins in services are paid onboarding and priority support. As a rule of thumb, start by charging 10 to 20 percent of your annual contract value so you can re-invest in the services you're providing (and carve out a little margin, too).

4. **Use the SaaS Services Planner™:** First, identify customer problems that are slowing your MRR growth that you can't solve with software. Then, create a repeatable process to solve a few of the most impactful ones. Finally, unlock the value by pricing your services with a margin target that aligns to your goals.

5. **MRR is king:** Use services to build your SaaS company, but don't let them become a distraction. Stay focused on solving problems that lead to retaining customers and increasing your MRR. If you need to discount something to get a deal done, sacrifice the services revenue and preserve your recurring revenue.

The Next Right Move

Write down a service you *already deliver to your customers* that you could start charging for today:

An existing service I'll start charging for is:

_____

The price I'll charge for this service will be:

_____

I'll start selling this service on this date:

_____

We've also put together a bunch of templates to help you nail this (the one around launching a setup fee is particularly awesome! It's been implemented by dozens of companies with incredible results.).

To snag the templates and examples, just head over to softwarebook.com/services. Trust us—this is some of the best stuff we've ever created.

One Last Story

"I knew we were doing the right things. I felt like we were incredibly close. But it didn't feel like anything was really happening... until it happened."

MADDIE BELL, co-founder and CEO of *Scheduler AI*

IF YOU'VE EVER LAUNCHED A SaaS company, built a product that you love, and spent a year or more in the "pain cave" trying to find product-market fit...that quote probably resonates. It was from Maddie Bell, the co-founder and CEO of Scheduler AI– and a SaaS Academy client who had recently graduated from our Accelerator program.

Maddie and her husband and co-founder Mike had created a proprietary AI technology that turns conversations into booked meetings—it was insanely powerful, and they knew it. They launched in 2022 and garnered quite a bit of attention...but attention doesn't pay the bills, and a year later they'd hit a Growth Ceiling at about $8,000 in MRR.

Their early traction quickly turned into an early plateau. And she needed to fix it if their company was going to survive.

She started by ruthlessly tracking the numbers for her Growth Ceiling Calculator (Current Customers, New Customers Per Month, Monthly Churn Rate, Monthly ARPA). In fact, she reviewed this every single Monday morning by entering them into a spreadsheet so she could gauge her progress. This weekly review kept her dialed in on which of the three controllable levers she needed to pull (ACQUISITION, RETENTION, EXPANSION)—in order to break through the ceiling.

Initially, she was marketing her company through almost every channel imaginable: earned media via podcast appearances, speaking engagements, SEO blog posts, co-marketing with other big brands, and some cold outbound prospecting as well. But once she started her weekly measurement, she realized that none of those efforts were actually driving leads—because she wasn't going deep enough. So, she dialed back everything except cold outbound via LinkedIn, which was brilliant, because this channel helped her learn the most about her customers in the shortest possible time (which in turn, helped her hone her positioning).

Those one-on-one conversations showed her something she didn't know before: There was a huge need for her technology inside of mid-market SaaS sales teams. Those teams had a lot to gain if her technology could get lost deals back on the calendar (which, of course, it could). She now had a solid "hot button issue" and an easy-to-understand First Value moment to push for.

The next obvious stop was pricing. Her initial offering was $49 per month, which felt crazy considering she was able to drive six-figure outcomes for her customers. So she worked through her pricing drivers and re-launched with a plan that charged *ten times that amount*—$499 per month. To her own surprise (but not ours), she was still closing deals.

She realized that she'd have to keep doing sales calls for the long haul, so her next move was to implement the Rocket Demo Builder™ framework to professionalize her sales process. Predictably, her close rates rose to well over 30 percent.

Everything was different now. She had a channel, a funnel, a sales process, a clear First Value Metric, and a pricing plan that made it all viable. Every deal she closed was worth at least ten of the deals she'd closed before, and her customers' ROI could actually be verified and shown back to them. Her new Growth Ceiling shot up about ten floors.

By early 2024, she had a completely different business—which went on to raise a multimillion-dollar investment round shortly thereafter.

Crazy, huh?

But that's what happens when you latch onto the one key principle we hope you took away from this book—the one that Maddie was grappling with every single Monday when she put her numbers into the Growth Ceiling Calculator:

> ## Your SaaS business is just a highly emotional math problem. And math problems have solutions.

Like Maddie and thousands of founders before her, you're going to reach a point where you feel like everything is broken. Where you feel like nothing you try is moving the needle, and somehow, you've managed to be both *incredibly busy* and *incredibly ineffective*.

It happens to all of us. Every business has survived a few near-death experiences.

But the path out of the "pain cave" is rooted in systems, not emotion. And now that you've got this book in your hands, you have all the core systems you need to fix *any* growth problem in any SaaS company.

Every time you think *it's not that simple* ...just come back to the math. Because it is that simple. *It's just not easy.*

***

When the four of us had a conversation about why we were writing this book, our biggest goal became clear—to show founders like you what's possible. We want you to understand that you're capable of building an incredible business on *your* terms.

Since this book's inception, our mission has always been to give founders one resource that clearly lays out the first principles that lead to repeatable success in software. Regardless of what software you sell, who you sell it to, or whether you choose to bootstrap or raise money, we know these frameworks are the timeless truths that drive the success of a recurring revenue business.

When you couple the company-building frameworks in this book with the frameworks from *Buy Back Your Time* that show you how to work efficiently and build a business you can run forever...you'll be completely unstoppable. That's what this is all about; putting the tools in your hands that create the optionality to build the business you want to build, the way you want to build it.

All that's left for you to do is apply what you've learned to your SaaS company.

Like we said in the beginning...we're rooting for you.

Dan, Matt, Johnny, and Marcel.

***

P.S.—If you're a B2B SaaS founder that liked what you read, we've got something more for you. Building a company can feel lonely, difficult, and confusing. Although reading this book is a good first step, we'd love to support you even more. We'd love for you to join us in SaaS Academy.

Our entire community is built around playbooks, templates, examples, and learning from people just like you...so you don't have to go it alone. The resources we've mentioned in this book are incredible, but if you want to go even faster, come join us. All you have to do is head over to softwarebook.com/help and fill out the form.

We'd love to learn about your business and see if we're a fit for each other.

Also, we couldn't write a book about channels and funnels and sales without having a call-to-action at the end, so there's that ;)

When You're Not Sure What to Do Next...Run the System

WE'RE LITERALLY GOING TO sum up this entire book in a few bullet points—and **we want you to put a bookmark on this page.** The next time you're feeling overwhelmed, you can come right back here, figure out which framework in this book will help you the most, and *go download the resources.* Fast action wins every time.

If you're feeling stuck:

First, do your math homework...

1. Calculate your Growth Ceiling using your four numbers to see your next plateau. (*softwarebook.com/ceiling*)

2. Run a couple of tests to see which of the three levers will deliver the biggest impact to the business. (*softwarebook.com/levers*)

LEVER I: ACQUISITION—If you need to Get More Customers...

1. **Is it an attention problem?** Audit your marketing channels and make sure you have at least one that's fully optimized. If not, fix it up before stacking on another channel. (*softwarebook.com/channels*)

2. **Is it a demand generation problem?** Review your funnel and make sure that you've got your Key Actions and Accelerants installed. If you have a choke point in the funnel, fix it to drive more leads down towards the point of sale. (*softwarebook.com/funnel*)

3. **Is it a sales problem?** Run the Rocket Demo Builder™ on your sales calls. Make sure you're not giving them a tour of every feature you've ever built. Ask for the deal, BAMFAM if you can't get it. (*softwarebook.com/demo*)

LEVER II: RETENTION—If you need to Keep Customers Longer...

1. **Is it an activation problem?** Make sure you know your First Value Metric and can get there in three steps or less. Find your biggest friction point and improve it. (*softwarebook.com/activation*)

2. **Is it a customer health problem?** Build a simple Customer Health Index and work to move people up on the scoreboard. Proactively reach out when you see a declining score so you can keep people happy. (*softwarebook.com/health*)

3. **Do you need more social proof?** Make sure you're tracking when customers win so you can make a quick ask—and do it in a way that makes *them* the hero of your story. (*softwarebook.com/ask*)

LEVER III: EXPANSION—If you need to Make Customers More Valuable...

1. **Is your pricing too low?** Run the Pricing Triangle to identify your Value Metric and some depth-of-usage drivers and/or feature fencing opportunities to drive EXPANSION. (*softwarebook.com/pricing*)

2. **Are you dragging your feet on a price increase?** Use the Ultimate Price-Increase Method™ to build your impact sheet and start deploying your updated pricing plans. (*softwarebook.com/increase*)

3.   **Can you add services to drive revenue?** Complete your Customer Journey Map exercise and look into paid implementation and/or priority support at a minimum. Your customers want you to help them win—bottom line. (*softwarebook.com/services*)

And last but not least...if you want to chat about how we can help...

Head over to softwarebook.com/help and drop us a line. We'd love to hear from you.

Thanks for reading. To find all the free resources in this book, you can go to softwarebook.com/resources

ABOUT THE AUTHORS

Dan Martell is the bestselling author of "Buy Back Your Time", founder of SaaS Academy, and the #1 executive coach for software CEOs in the world. After building, scaling, and exiting three tech companies, he became an angel investor and trusted mentor for tech entrepreneurs globally. As a passionate advocate for entrepreneurial education, Dan's content, keynotes, and coaching programs have helped thousands of clients unlock growth in their businesses and lives.

Matt Verlaque is the COO of SaaS Academy, where he helps train and coach hundreds of B2B SaaS founders to build the company of their dreams. After over a decade of service in the fire department, he "accidentally" started his first SaaS company UpLaunch in 2016 and served as its CEO through a successful acquisition in 2020. Outside of his work, Matt's a devoted husband, a loving father of three sons, and spends his spare time weightlifting, running, and writing.

Johnny Page is an intrapreneur at heart. He spent 7 years climbing the ladder from sales rep to CEO at Silvertrac, taking the company through an exit to K1 Investments in 2019. In 2020, he joined Dan Martell as a coach at SaaS Academy. Today, Johnny is now a partner and the CEO of SaaS Academy, using his experience as both a client and coach to help founders scale to their Perfect Exit.

Marcel Petitpas is the strategic guru at SaaS Academy, where he's coached over 600 B2B SaaS companies around the world. From his formative tech years at Apple, he's now the founder behind Parakeeto, building the future of how we measure and improve the profitability of professional services. Beyond business, Marcel is an avid bio hacker, fitness enthusiast, and part-time beekeeper.

***

SaaS Academy is the #1 training and coaching program for B2B SaaS founders in the world, with thousands of founders coached and dozens of Perfect Exits™ created. For more information about SaaS Academy, head over to saasacademy.com.

SOURCES

[i] Noah Kagan, *Million Dollar Weekend: The Surprisingly Simple Way to Launch a 7-Figure Business in 48 Hours*

[ii] Jason Fried and David Heinemeier Hansson, *Rework*

[iii] https://www.youtube.com/watch?v=-PZouDwpIYQ

[iv] https://investors.shopify.com/news-and-events/press-releases/news-details/2024/Shopify-Announces-Fourth-Quarter-and-Full-Year-2023-Financial-Results/default.aspx

[v] Dave Gerhardt, Twitter

[vi] https://www.saastr.com/every-marketing-initiative-every-channel-plateaus-plan-for-it/

[vii] Source: Gupta Media's Meta CPM Tracker, which tracks historical CPMs over millions of data points in a Looker Studio instance. The URL is a beast, so we recommend searching for it if you want to have a look.

[viii] Mark Roberge, *The Sales Acceleration Formula: Using Data, Technology, and Inbound Selling to go from $0 to $100 Million*

[ix] https://baremetrics.com/blog/customer-feedback-to-fuel-growth

[x] https://baremetrics.com/blog/how-we-reduced-churn#:~:text=Just%20by%20reducing%20churn%2C%20not,focusing%20on%20fixing%20right%20now.

[xi] https://www.youtube.com/watch?v=nqXhyibbfyQ

[xii] https://www.sequoiacap.com/article/notion-spotlight/
https://www.news.aakashg.com/p/how-notion-grows

[xiii] https://www.cnbc.com/2024/05/14/notion-cnbc-disruptor-50.html#:~:text=More%20coverage%20of%20the%202024%20CNBC%20Disruptor

%2050&text=For%20a%20company%20with%20an,and%20a%20centralized%20ow
nership%20structure.

[xiv] https://hackernoon.com/community-led-growth-the-story-of-notion-and-
its-$10-billion-growth-engine

[xv] https://psycnet.apa.org/record/1972-22883-001

[xvi] https://www.precursive.com/post/the-role-of-professional-services-in-saas-
companies

www.ingramcontent.com/pod-product-compliance
Lightning Source LLC
La Vergne TN
LVHW091533210625
814371LV00007B/116/J